NAVIGATING YOUR
SMALL
BUSINESS
FINANCES

How to Establish Financial Operations, Interpret Reports, and Drive Strategic Growth

Also by Amanda J. Painter
The Team Solution Series: HR Coaching to Grow Teams and Profit

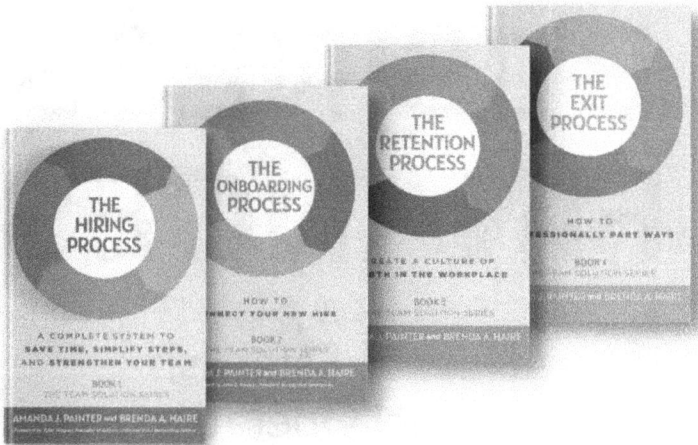

This series offers tools, systems, and strategies to guide you through every stage of the employee journey: hiring, onboarding, retention, and exit.

NAVIGATING YOUR
SMALL BUSINESS FINANCES

How to Establish Financial Operations, Interpret Reports, and Drive Strategic Growth

AMANDA J. PAINTER

Joy of PURSUIT
PUBLISHING

Navigating Your Small Business Finances
© 2025 Amanda J. Painter

Published by Joy of Pursuit Publishing

Maryville, Tennessee 37803

JoyofPursuitPublishing.com

Library of Congress Cataloging: 2025900580

Softcover: 978-1-957205-12-0

Hardcover: 978-1-957205-13-7

E-book: 978-1-957205-11-3

Available in hardcover, softcover, and e-book.

The Small Business Finance Toolbox

Build a solid foundation with this FREE resource.

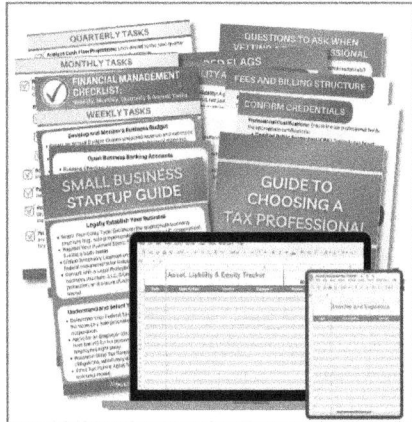

What's included?

- Small Business Startup Guide
- Income and Expense Tracking Template
- Asset, Liability & Equity Tracking Template
- Financial Management Checklists: Monthly, Quarterly, and Annual Tasks
- Guide to Choosing a Tax Professional

Scan here for your free download or visit tools.thejoyofpursuit.com/financetoolbox

Disclaimer

This book is designed to help small business owners with the basics of financial management. Use of this book does not constitute accounting or legal advice and does not establish any kind of accountant-client or attorney-client relationship. The information provided herein is for informational and educational purposes only. It is not intended to replace professional legal or tax advice. Making adjustments to a financial strategy or plan should only be undertaken after consulting with appropriate legal and financial professionals.

Given the ever-changing nature of U.S. laws, business owners should seek appropriate legal counsel to ensure compliance with the latest local and federal regulations. Neither Joy of Pursuit Publishing nor the author are responsible for any failure to comply with these laws, nor do they guarantee financial results obtained from using this book.

As this book is distributed globally, some information may only apply to business laws and regulations within the United States. Business owners in other countries should conduct their own research to comply with applicable laws. Neither Joy of Pursuit Publishing nor the author assumes responsibility for non-compliance.

Contents

Introduction

Are you prepared to beat the odds?

According to the U.S. Bureau of Labor Statistics, about 20 percent of small businesses fail within their first year, and nearly 50 percent don't survive past the fifth year.[1] In a study published by the U.S. Chamber of Commerce, it is reported that a staggering 82 percent of business failures stem from poor cash flow management.[2]

While businesses can fail for numerous reasons, one thing is certain: without mastering your finances, your business will not survive long-term. You cannot outrun or outperform financial chaos; it's a challenge you must face head-on.

If you're holding this book, chances are you're

- a small business owner,

- a side-hustler,

- a freelancer, or

- someone with entrepreneurial dreams while working for someone else.

You're likely an expert in your field—that's why you've already ventured into your own business or are planning to take the leap.

But are you an expert at bookkeeping and interpreting financial data?

If you answered "no," don't worry. You don't have to abandon all your entrepreneurial hopes and dreams if you're not a numbers person. But you *do* need to improve your financial literacy, and with the right instruction, you *can*. Read on to learn more.

Accounting is the backbone of a successful business, no matter the size. Cash flow is your company's lifeline. Without a clear understanding of where your money comes from and where it goes, survival and growth will be hard to come by, if not impossible. This is why comprehension of your financial reports is critical, for they are the key to assessing the health of your business.

Whether you're about to launch or you're scaling up, a strong financial foundation is a must. It will drive your decisions on pricing, hiring, marketing, and overall business strategy.

As a small business owner, managing the finances can feel overwhelming. Tasks like tracking expenses, reconciling accounts, and forecasting cash flow are daunting and time-consuming. With so much on your plate—building your brand, purchasing inventory, and meeting with clients—it's tempting to put your finances on the back burner.

But here's the truth: neglecting your finances puts you on a fast track to failure. Regardless of the type of business you run, accurate and timely bookkeeping is nonnegotiable if you're going to succeed. To get ahead, you must prioritize financial literacy, leverage tools (such as accounting software), and know when to bring in professionals and streamline your systems.

Starting a business is no easy feat; it's demanding, stressful, and filled with uncertainty. But working for yourself, building something from the ground up, and pursuing your dreams—there is joy in that! And it's a joy that is unmatched when working for someone else.

Are you willing to invest the effort required to maintain that sense of fulfillment? Are you prepared to gain the knowledge to effectively oversee your small business finances and secure lasting success?

That's why I wrote this book—to be your go-to guide for navigating the financial side of your business. My passion is to help small business owners like you thrive, and the insights found within these pages will help you do just that.

This book is your roadmap to understanding your finances, from profit and loss statements to balance sheets and cash flow management. Regardless of where you are in your business journey, you'll gain practical tools and clear explanations to assist you in making smarter, data-driven decisions. Enhancing your financial literacy will simplify the complex world of small business finance and empower you to make strategic choices about pricing, marketing, and operations, which will in turn drive growth and profitability.

This isn't just about the basics; it's about avoiding costly mistakes by learning from others' experiences. But don't be intimidated. This book is written in an easy-to-follow format with user-friendly tips. Even if numbers aren't your thing, you'll walk away with the confidence to handle your finances well, work effectively with your tax professionals, and propel your business forward.

Whether you're just starting or have been in business for years, this book provides the knowledge and structure you need. If you're at the beginning of your journey, you've picked it up at the perfect time. For those of you who are already running a business, I encourage you to explore the Table of Contents, identify your most pressing challenges, and start there. Then, you can dive deeper into the rest of the book to ensure that you fully grasp every component of the accounting process.

This book is structured in three parts: First, we'll cover the fundamentals of small business finances. Next, we'll explore bookkeeping essentials, helping you stay organized and in control. Finally, we'll pull it all together with accounting practices that will provide insight to drive your strategy forward. Each chapter ends with key takeaways, and a detailed index at the back of the book allows you to quickly locate answers whenever you need them. Also, be sure to download The Small Business Finances Toolbox for additional tools and insights to simplify and optimize your company's financial management.

Let's start your journey to business finance success!

Scan to download your FREE Small Business Finances Toolbox or visit: tools.thejoyofpursuit.com/financetoolbox

Fundamentals

Before you can effectively tackle bookkeeping for your business, you must first establish a solid foundation of fundamental business and accounting knowledge. This starts with an awareness of the most common mistakes small business owners make and how you can proactively avoid costly errors. Familiarizing yourself with these potential pitfalls will better prepare you to establish efficient and effective bookkeeping practices from the start.

Launching a new business involves critical decisions, from choosing your entity type to determining your tax classification. These foundational steps directly affect your bookkeeping and financial reporting obligations, making it crucial that you get them right.

Beyond the business setup, understanding core accounting principles—including assets, liabilities, equity, revenue, and expenses—is imperative for recording business transactions accurately. A solid grasp of these concepts strengthens your financial literacy and allows you to maintain your books properly.

Equally important is an awareness of the roles and responsibilities of key players, including you—the business owner—the bookkeeper, the accountant, and the tax professionals. Many entrepreneurs like to fly solo and try to handle everything themselves, but the reality is, you can't do it all. It's common not to know exactly who you should hire to accomplish certain financial tasks. Clarifying who handles jobs like payroll, invoicing, tax prep, and financial reporting allows you to prioritize your efforts and know when to seek expert advice. This clear division of duties supports the scrupulous upkeep of compliant financial records.

With this foundation, you'll be better positioned to implement bookkeeping practices that drive long-term financial health and success.

In the upcoming chapters, you will find answers to these pressing questions:

- What records should I keep?

- Do I need accounting software?

- Can I handle bookkeeping myself?

- What is the difference between an entity type and tax classification?

- What is the difference between bookkeeping and accounting?

- What are the pros and cons of cash-basis versus accrual accounting?

- What are the roles of different financial professionals, and which are recommended?

- How do I find the right tax professional for my business?

Chapter One

Avoiding Costly Mistakes

Throughout my career of working with small businesses, I have encountered countless bookkeeping mistakes. While some are easy to rectify, others are so substantial that it is more efficient to start over than attempt to sort out the mess. In this chapter, I highlight some of the most common errors I've seen and provide proactive measures to steer clear of them.

Mistake #1: No Filing System

Inadequate record-keeping practices—such as haphazardly storing receipts, invoices, and bank statements—can lead to missing or incomplete financial data, complicating the reconciliation of accounts and producing erroneous financial reports.

Establishing a systematic filing system should be a high priority; simply stashing paper receipts in a box or letting digital receipts accumulate in your email inbox is insufficient. Decide on a structured approach, whether it involves organizing digital folders, uploading receipts to accounting software, or utilizing another method. Determine a regular schedule for filing, whether it's at the end of each week or during the final fifteen minutes of each workday.

Once you create your system, you must follow through with the implementation of it. This requires self-discipline. Spending time digitizing receipts and paper invoices pays off when it comes time to retrieve a document. Physical papers are prone to be misplaced, damaged, or misfiled, while digital files are more reliable and accessible (especially when backed up to a cloud or an external storage drive).

Spending a few minutes filing each week can prevent the loss of receipts and possible financial setbacks over time. Although the odds of an audit may be slim, disorganized records can turn an audit into a massive headache with potentially negative outcomes.

What records should I keep?

Save every document related to your business finances. This includes invoices, receipts, bank and credit card statements, tax returns, and other documents detailing income, expenses, deductions, or credits—basically anything with a number on it. Retain these records for at least three years beyond the tax filing season to comply with regulatory requirements.

Mistake #2: No Accounting Software

Small businesses often operate with limited resources, including funds and personnel. As a result, you may not have the budget to invest in sophisticated accounting software. So how do you manage finances effectively?

While they have their merits, relying solely on spreadsheets for bookkeeping is outdated. (I do love a good spreadsheet, though!) Once, I was brought in to consult with a company that used only a spreadsheet to track finances, despite substantial revenues of more than $10 million and $2 million in the preceding years. This makeshift method of using a spreadsheet, although impressive, led to chaos.

The business owners were unfamiliar with basic accounting principles. Their disorganization and lack of a balance sheet had their CPA on the verge of firing them. Disputes between partners over financial matters occurred frequently. Although revenue was flowing in, the absence of a proper system for analyzing the numbers was evident in their business strategy.

This story underscores the necessity of accounting software. Now, you might not want to choose your accounting software at the inception of your business. During this initial period, starting with a spreadsheet is advisable. (Download The Small Business Finances Toolbox for a template to get you started.) However, as your business grows, transitioning to software will provide significant ease and benefits while reducing human error.

Even the smallest businesses can benefit from automated bookkeeping solutions. Popular options for small businesses in the United States include QuickBooks and Xero. However, you may not require such advanced software immediately. Free alternatives are available, but they are typically only suitable for companies with very simple bookkeeping needs.

There is a learning curve with any software, just as there is with running a business. Implementing a solid accounting system is a foundational component of establishing a legitimate business.

Mistake #3: No Sense of Urgency

Finances often fall into Quadrant 2—Important/Not Urgent—of the Eisenhower Matrix.[3] Neglecting them for too long can escalate the priority to the Important/Urgent quadrant—think tax time and loss of sleep.

Prioritize tracking your business's financial information throughout the year by scheduling dedicated time for this task. Details are vital, and bookkeeping is a meticulous job. Errors and bad financial habits can jeopardize your business and cause unnecessary stress.

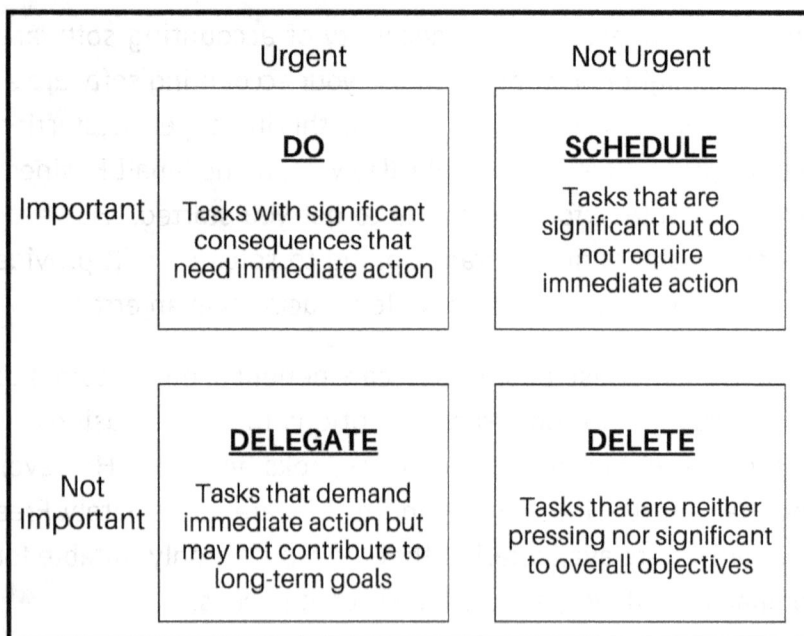

	Urgent	Not Urgent
Important	**DO** Tasks with significant consequences that need immediate action	**SCHEDULE** Tasks that are significant but do not require immediate action
Not Important	**DELEGATE** Tasks that demand immediate action but may not contribute to long-term goals	**DELETE** Tasks that are neither pressing nor significant to overall objectives

If you've fallen behind, catch up now. (Refer to Chapter 9 for the steps to take.) Avoid procrastination when it comes to organizing your finances, and resist the temptation to postpone catching up until the end of the year. Bookkeeping is not a task just for tax season. Staying up to date with your business finances simplifies tax preparation and keeps you well-informed about your company's financial health.

Mistake #4: DIY Bookkeeping

Many small business owners mistakenly believe they can handle bookkeeping without specialized training. (Odds are, if you're reading this book, you do not have a financial background.) The reality is that small technical mistakes can snowball into significant discrepancies in the books. These errors can result in incorrect tax filings, among other complications.

Here are the top challenges that arise when attempting a do-it-yourself approach to bookkeeping:

- Lack of Accounting Knowledge—not understanding basic accounting principles can lead to errors in recording transactions and the misclassification of expenses, which result in unreliable financial statements. Even with accounting software, relying solely on it without grasping the underlying principles can cause data-entry mistakes, report misinterpretation, and inadequate financial analysis.

- Neglecting to Reconcile—failure to conduct regular bank reconciliations can result in discrepancies between bank balances and book balances, leading to incomplete financial reporting and mismanagement of cash flow.

- Overlooking Tax Complexities—ignoring the need for professional accounting support or failing to fully comprehend tax obligations (e.g., proper withholding, reporting, and remittance) can lead to penalties, fines, and legal issues. Professional advice is indispensable when navigating complex accounting issues, tax matters, and regulatory compliance; it's also beneficial for identifying potential tax savings.

Outsourcing bookkeeping to qualified professionals can provide you peace of mind and ensure accurate and compliant financials. (This subject will be covered in more detail in Chapter 4, which explains the various roles and responsibilities necessary for bookkeeping and accounting.)

Mistake #5: Ignoring Financial Statements

Neglecting to review and analyze financial statements regularly is a common pitfall, resulting in a significant lack of insight into the business's overall financial health and performance. This lack of awareness can hinder strategic planning for the company's future.

Financial statements—balance sheets, profit and loss statements, and cash flow statements—provide a comprehensive view of a business's financial position, profitability, and liquidity. Consistently reviewing these documents allows you to pinpoint areas of strength, weaknesses, opportunities, and potential risks. Without this critical financial information, it becomes extremely challenging to decide on investments, expenditures, pricing, hiring, and other strategic initiatives.

Prioritize the time required to review your company's financial reports. This includes analyzing key performance indicators, identifying trends, and investigating anomalies or areas of concern. By staying closely attuned to your business finances, you can proactively make strategic adjustments and support long-term sustainability.

Mistake #6: Mixing Business and Personal Funds

Using business accounts for personal purchases, and vice versa, is known as commingling funds. DO NOT COMMINGLE PERSONAL AND BUSINESS FUNDS! I cannot stress this enough. This is one of the most frequent mistakes I've seen business owners make. When you own a business, it's tempting to view its assets as your own. However, blurring the lines between business and personal money can pose serious financial and legal risks for both you and your business.

To avoid these issues, maintain a separate bank account and credit card for your business. Even if you're a sole proprietor, resist the mindset of "it all passes through to me at tax time anyway." Below are several reasons why maintaining a clear distinction between personal and business finances is essential.

Accurate Accounting

Keeping personal and business finances separate ensures that your financial records are reliable and streamlines your bookkeeping and accounting processes. Precise records allow you to easily reconcile accounts, identify discrepancies, and address issues that may arise. This clarity allows you to correctly assess the financial health of your business, monitor cash flow, and effectively strategize.

Cost Savings

Distinguishing between business and personal transactions for every transaction each month can be a time-consuming and costly endeavor, especially if you outsource your bookkeeping. I've heard clients say, "But I get good cash-back rewards on this card," or tout discounts and other perks to justify using the same account for business and personal expenses. While these incentives are appealing, the truth is that these benefits do not offset the costs associated with having a bookkeeper sort and categorize each individual transaction.

Also, your time is incredibly valuable. Having to review and explain every single transaction every month diverts your attention away from business matters that require your expertise. The time lost on mundane tasks often outweighs any perceived rewards of using a business card for personal expenses.

Ultimately, the administrative hassle and financial drain of mixing personal and business expenses will outweigh any marginal rewards program or discount. Maintaining clear separation between the two is a more efficient and cost-effective approach in the long run.

Tax Compliance

Separating personal and business finances simplifies tax reporting and compliance. It supports error-free record-keeping for tax deductions and adherence to tax laws and regulations. Mixing personal and business transactions complicates tax filings and increases the risk of errors, audits, and penalties.

Legal Protection

Maintaining separate accounts for personal and business finances protects your personal assets from business liabilities. Ideally, if you have a clear line of separation and legal action is ever taken against you, claimants may only be able to access assets held in the business's name—not your personal assets.

Commingling personal and business funds can destroy the protection of a corporate structure that should shield you from personal liability. Demonstrating that a business owner has mixed personal funds with business assets can "pierce the corporate veil," exposing your personal assets to the liability of legal action.

Professionalism

Maintaining separate accounts conveys professionalism and legitimacy to clients, customers, investors, employees, and other stakeholders. It demonstrates that you take your business seriously and adhere to sound financial practices, enhancing your credibility and reputation. Additionally, if you serve as a fiduciary for the business or have a business partner, misappropriating business funds for personal expenses can violate ethical and legal obligations, damaging trust and relationships.

It bears repeating: commingling funds leads to issues and costs down the line. Every client I've worked with who commingled has faced significant problems. If you're currently mixing personal and business finances, create a plan now to disentangle. Keeping your accounts separate is a fundamental practice, to promote financial stability, accountability, and success for small business owners.

What about start-up costs before I have a business bank account?

This happens in almost every business, and it can be accounted for in your bookkeeping. Keep all receipts and detailed records of these expenses.

You can account for start-up costs in one of two ways:

Reimbursement

Once you have your business bank account set up (and enough funds to reimburse yourself), you will pay yourself back and record the transaction with all the details of the expenses incurred. (This will resemble an expense report.)

Owner Investment

You can consider these start-up expenses as part of your owner contribution (capital investment) to the company. (See Chapter 7 for more on owner contributions.) With this method, you will record the details of the expense transactions and indicate the funding source as an owner contribution. This will show the expenses on your profit and loss statement (P&L) and increase your owner's equity on the balance sheet. The equity can be withdrawn at a future date.

Chapter Highlights

Take these actions to avoid the most common small business finance mistakes:

- Establish a filing and financial tracking system.

- Utilize accounting software.

- Prioritize bookkeeping tasks.

- Hire a professional when needed.

- Review your financial statements consistently.

- Avoid using business accounts for personal purchases.

Chapter Two

Defining Your Business

You'll need to determine some specific details about your business before you set up an accounting system. Your business model, entity type, and federal tax classification impact a multitude of items and actions: accounting methods, tax filings, how you pay yourself, which reports to review, and more.

What follows is a high-level overview of how to define your business, but it is by no means fully inclusive of all the nuances involved. Consult with a tax professional to determine the most suitable business entity and tax classification for your business.

Entity Types and Federal Classifications

Be aware that federal tax classifications can differ from the type of business entity you create at the state level. Federal tax classifications determine how the IRS assesses a business's taxes. Entity types refer to the legal structure of the business and how it is established in your state.

Selecting the right type of entity and federal classification is paramount and among the initial decisions an entrepreneur makes when launching a small business. Each business structure offers unique benefits and drawbacks concerning liability protection, tax implications, management flexibility, and regulatory obligations. Factors such as business nature, size, ownership structure, and long-term objectives play pivotal roles in determining the most appropriate business structure.

To create a legitimate business, apply for a federal tax identification number (also known as an employer identification number or EIN) in the United States. During this process, you will select the type of tax classification for your business. This designation determines how your business will be taxed and regulated at a federal level.

Carefully consider your options and consult with legal and tax professionals to choose the classification best suited to your business. Do know that in certain circumstances you can change your classification. This most often happens when sole proprietorships and partnerships become established and choose to elect an S-corp status (see "S Corporation").

Here are the most common classifications for small businesses, with a brief explanation of each:

Sole Proprietorship

The simplest business structure is a sole proprietorship. This is the most common structure for a small business (especially when newly formed) owned and operated by a single individual. The owner has full control over the business, will receive all the profits, and is personally liable for all debts. Tax obligations pass through to the owner's personal tax return. Sole proprietorships are easy to establish and require minimal paperwork.

Partnership

A partnership is similar to a sole proprietorship except that two or more individuals share ownership. The owners report their share of business income and expenses on their personal tax returns, the same as a sole proprietorship. Partnerships are relatively easy to establish and offer flexibility in terms of management and decision-making.

While there are several types of partnerships, the main ones are general and limited partnerships. In a general partnership, all partners share ownership and management responsibilities. In a limited partnership, one or more general partners run the business, and one or more limited partners contribute capital but have limited involvement with the operations of the business.

S Corporation (S Corp)

An S corp is a business structure that elects to pass corporate income, losses, and deductions through to its shareholders for federal tax purposes. S corps are popular among small businesses (once they have established consistent revenue) because they offer the benefits of limited liability protection to shareholders and pass-through taxation, allowing business income to be taxed at the individual shareholder level. Typically, the owner(s) of an S corp receives a salary. This salary must be a "reasonable compensation" rate for the services provided to the business, and it is subject to payroll taxes.

S corp owners must work with a tax professional to determine an appropriate salary level based on factors such as industry standards, job responsibilities, experience, and location. This supports compliance with IRS regulations and avoids potential tax penalties related to underpayment of payroll taxes.

C Corporation (C Corp)

A C corp is a legal entity owned by shareholders but taxed as a separate entity. The shareholders are not personally liable for the corporation's debts and liabilities. C corps offer the most limited liability protection but are subject to more taxation: business profits are taxed at the corporate level, and dividends distributed to shareholders are taxed again at the individual level. C corps are often preferred for businesses seeking to raise capital through public stock offerings or venture capital investments.

What about a Limited Liability Company (LLC)?

An LLC is not a recognized business classification for federal tax purposes. It is a type of business entity formed at the state level. It is a hybrid business structure, combining the limited liability protection of a corporation with the pass-through taxation of a sole proprietorship or partnership. Most LLCs have the tax classification of a sole proprietorship or partnership, though an LLC can elect to be taxed as an S or C corp.

Again, consult with a tax professional to determine which type of business entity and tax classification is best for your business.

Business Model

When establishing your business, familiarize yourself with different business models to determine where yours fits. Your business model outlines how you intend to generate profit. The business model you choose will affect your financial processes and accounting method. (See "Accounting Methods" in the next chapter.)

The following are some of the most prevalent business models for small businesses, though this list is not exhaustive:

Manufacturing

A manufacturing business model involves producing goods for sale by acquiring raw materials, manufacturing products, and then selling to distributors, retailers, and/or end consumers. This process includes managing cost of goods sold (COGS), which encompasses materials purchased, labor costs, and freight expenses, as well as inventory for both raw materials and finished products awaiting sale.

We often associate manufacturers with large production facilities, but this is not always the case. Examples of small manufacturing businesses include candle making, jewelry crafting, 3D printing, woodworking, and more.

Retail

Retailers are often the final link in the supply chain, purchasing goods from manufacturers or distributors and then selling them to customers at higher prices to cover expenses and generate profit. A retailer may specialize in a specific niche or offer a diverse range of products. This model spans various industries, from clothing and food vendors to department stores, automotive dealerships, and e-commerce platforms.

Service Provider

A service provider offers services to consumers and/or other businesses, for example, landscaping, computer repair, and consulting. Unlike businesses with inventory, service providers do not typically maintain stock but can incur cost of sales such as travel, equipment, supplies, and labor expenses.

Operating in this business model involves charging a predetermined fee for a specific service. The service provider can enhance its revenue streams by serving more clients or adjusting its rates. Depending on the nature of the services provided, the business may bill clients based on hourly rates, monthly retainers, or a predetermined fee schedule.

Construction

Construction businesses undertake tasks related to the construction, renovation, or restoration of residential, commercial, or industrial properties. Examples of these entities are general contracting, home remodeling, plumbing, electrical work, or roofing. A construction business is sometimes viewed as a hybrid of a manufacturer and a service provider due to its blended offerings of tangible product creation and intangible service delivery.

Other types of businesses exist, including some that are combinations of the above-mentioned. Throughout this book, I'll use three fictitious businesses to provide examples, highlighting the financial specifics of each. Here they are listed, along with their tax classifications and type of business model:

1. Joe's Woodworking

   ○ Structure: Sole Proprietor

   ○ Model: Manufacturing

2. A&J's Boutique

   ○ Structure: Partnership

   ○ Model: Retail

3. The Marketing Group

   ○ Structure: S Corporation

   ○ Model: Service Provider

B2B vs. B2C

Business-to-business (B2B) and business-to-consumer (B2C) are two distinct business models, each targeting a different type of customer. Here's an overview of their differences and how they influence a company's financials:

B2B (Business-to-Business)

- Target Audience—sells products or services to other businesses

- Pricing—often negotiated and varies based on contracts, order volume, and client needs

- Order Size and Frequency—involves larger, recurring orders, resulting in more predictable revenue

- Revenue Pattern—generally stable due to long-term contracts, but losing a major client may significantly affect earnings

- Cash Flow—longer payment terms (e.g., "net 30"), which may delay income and require careful cash flow management to maintain liquidity

B2C (Business-to-Consumer)

- Target Audience—sells directly to individual consumers

- Pricing—usually fixed, focusing on competitive pricing, discounts, and promotions

- Order Size and Frequency—smaller, often one-time purchases, though repeat business remains important

- Revenue Pattern—more volatile due to consumer spending behaviors and seasonality, but a broad customer base reduces the burden of losing individual customers

- Cash Flow—mostly immediate payments but requires careful oversight of inventory and awareness of customer demand

The differences between the B2B and B2C models influence revenue, accounts payable, and cash flow. Awareness of the unique dynamics of each model is essential for optimizing financial strategies and achieving sustainable growth.

Chapter Highlights

- Business Structure Impact—the choice of business model, entity type, and federal tax classification influences how you handle finances, file taxes, and structure your accounting system.

- Entities and Classifications—being familiar with the difference between state-level business entities and federal tax classifications is crucial for tax compliance and liability protection.

- Common Business Structures—sole proprietorships, partnerships, S corps, and C corps each offer unique benefits and challenges in terms of control, liability, and tax implications.

- LLCs—while not a federal tax classification, an LLC offers flexibility, combining liability protection with various tax options, including sole proprietorship, partnership, or corporation status.

- Business Models and Accounting—your business model (manufacturing, retail, or service provider) dictates the financial processes and accounting methods required for your business.

- B2B vs. B2C—distinguishing between B2B and B2C models helps guide pricing strategies, revenue patterns, and cash flow effectively.

- Professional Advice—seek guidance from tax and legal professionals to choose the best structure and tax classification for your business.

Chapter Three

Accounting Basics
and Financial
Literacy

To accurately assess your company's financial health, a general knowledge of basic accounting principles is required. In this chapter, I'll cover foundational concepts, provide a list of terms, and highlight synonymous terms for easy reference.

Accounting vs. Bookkeeping

Although the words *bookkeeping* and *accounting* are often used interchangeably, they represent distinct but interconnected processes within financial administration. Bookkeeping focuses on the systematic recording and organization of all financial transactions and comprises the tracking of income, expenses, assets, liabilities, and equity. It ensures that every transaction is documented and categorized correctly, which supports the maintenance of clear and up-to-date financial records. (Bookkeeping is covered in Part 2 of this book.)

Accounting, on the other hand, encompasses a much broader scope (covered in Part 3). It builds upon the data collected through bookkeeping to analyze, interpret, and summarize financial information. This process involves the generation of financial reports, forecasts, and analyses to provide usable data. Accounting enables informed strategic planning and compliance with regulatory requirements. While bookkeeping is about capturing financial data, accounting transforms the data into meaningful insights that guide business decisions.

Financial administration for your small business will include both bookkeeping and accounting practices.

Accounting Methods

All businesses use an accounting method for bookkeeping and tax filings. This method is a set of rules to be followed when recording financial transactions. These rules instruct the business on how to recognize, measure, and report revenue, expenses, assets, liabilities, and equity. The two primary methods of accounting are cash basis and accrual.

Cash Basis

In cash-basis accounting, transactions (both incoming and outgoing) are recorded when money changes hands (physically or digitally). This means that revenue isn't recorded until funds are received, not when a service is provided, expenses are incurred, or work is completed. Expense transactions are recorded only when cash is paid out.

Pros

Cash-basis accounting is relatively uncomplicated. The ease of implementing this method makes it popular among small businesses and sole proprietors. It provides a clear picture of how much cash the business has on hand at any given time. From a bookkeeping perspective, the bulk of the work is matching and/or categorizing transactions once they occur. This decreases the amount of manual input required, thus saving resources.

Cons

Though it is easy to implement and follow, this method fails to reflect the true financial performance of some businesses and may distort the reality of the business's financial position. For example, a company with sizeable long-term contracts may incur significant expenses upfront, but payment may not be made until the work is complete or specific milestones are met (depending on the terms of the contract). Since the anticipated revenue isn't recorded until payment is received, it may look like the company isn't profitable in the meantime.

Accrual

With the accrual accounting method, transactions are recorded when they occur, regardless of when money is exchanged. This means that revenue is recorded when it's earned, even if payment hasn't yet been received, and expenses are recorded when they're incurred, even if they are not yet paid for. For example, if you are a consultant and provide your client with a consultation session, you would record the revenue from that session on the date it was provided (and likely the date the invoice is sent), even though you have not received payment for the consultation yet.

Pros

Accrual accounting can provide a more reliable picture of a business's financial performance and position over time. It matches anticipated receivables with the expenses incurred to generate the specific revenue, giving a better understanding of financial obligations and profitability.

Cons

This accounting method is more complex than the cash-basis method, making it more time-consuming and costly. Recording transactions when incurred rather than when money is exchanged may require estimates, adjustments for accrued items, and more manual input overall in your bookkeeping.

Another downside to the accrual method is the discrepancy in cash flow versus the recognition of revenue. For example, you may recognize the revenue of a substantial long-term contract, but the reality may be that you do not have the cash on hand to use for expenses.

Which method should I choose?

As you've read, each method has its pros and cons. The accounting method you choose will depend on multiple factors. The first is the size of your business. If you're reading this, you are likely in the small business realm, and cash-basis accounting will probably be the best for you (but not in every situation). Before committing to it, be sure you know what the industry standards are for your type of company. Also, research regulatory requirements and consult with a tax professional to be certain you understand the tax implications of accrual versus cash basis.

Once you select the accounting method for your business, you must use it consistently from one accounting period to the next to sustain comparability and accuracy in your financial reporting.

Accounting Standards and Principles

Federal Accounting Standards Board (FASB)

The Federal Accounting Standards Board, or FASB, is the governing body responsible for establishing financial accounting and reporting standards in the United States. The board aims to standardize financial reporting by private sector entities, ensuring the delivery of relevant and informative information to investors and others using financial reports.

Generally Accepted Accounting Principles (GAAP)

The Generally Accepted Accounting Principles (GAAP) are a set of guidelines and practices established by the FASB for financial accounting and reporting. (Visit fasb.org for more information.) These fundamental principles are widely used in the United States to direct the preparation and presentation of financial statements, ensuring consistency and transparency in financial reporting.

GAAP includes ten basic principles:

1. Principle of Regularity—the business's accounting must strictly adhere to the GAAP standards for all financial information.

2. Principle of Consistency—the business's accounting practices are both consistent and comparable in each reporting period.

3. Principle of Sincerity—the business's accountants are committed to the authenticity and objectivity of financial reporting without bias.

4. Principle of Permanence of Methods—the business's accounting practices are consistent throughout the preparation of all financial reports.

5. Principle of Non-Compensation—regardless of whether the business's performance is positive or negative, all aspects of its financial performance are reported.

6. Principle of Prudence—all of the business's accounting entries are fact-based, free of speculation, realistic, and timely.

7. Principle of Continuity—it is assumed that the business will remain in operation based on its asset valuations.

8. Principle of Periodicity—the business's accounting periods are routine and consistent (i.e., divided by fiscal quarters or fiscal years).

9. Principle of Materiality—all of the data in the financial reports are based on factual information to fully disclose the business's monetary position, and assets are valued at cost.

10. Principle of Utmost Good Faith—all of those involved in the business's accounting process are truthful and honest in all reports and transactions.

List of Terms

Accounting Period

An accounting period is the time frame in which a business completes its accounting cycle. Typically lasting one year, this period allows businesses to record all transactions to produce financial statements and reconcile all transactions with bank statements. Most small businesses use the calendar year, but you may also establish a fiscal year for your accounting period (see "Fiscal Year" below). The primary purpose is to provide a consistent schedule for financial reporting, enabling businesses to compare performance over different periods, analyze trends, and meet regulatory requirements.

Amortization

Amortization is the distribution of the cost of an intangible asset, such as an intellectual property right, over its projected useful life.

Balance Sheet

This essential financial report provides a snapshot of a company's financial position at a specific point in time. It is comprised of the company's assets, liabilities, and equity, showing what the company owns and owes, as well as the owners' stake. The balance sheet reveals the company's financial health. (This will be covered in depth in Chapter 11.)

Chart of Accounts (COA)

This is a comprehensive list of all the accounts you use for recording financial transactions, including assets, liabilities, equity, revenue, and expenses (more on this in Part 2).

Credits and Debits

For each accounting transaction, an account from your COA will be debited (subtracted from) and another credited (added to).

Depreciation

Depreciation is the distribution of the cost of a tangible asset over its useful life, which reflects its decreasing value as it is used and/or ages.

Double-entry Accounting

Double-entry accounting is a bookkeeping method in which each transaction impacts at least two accounts, ensuring debits and credits are always balanced. This system mitigates accounting errors and is used by companies of all sizes. It is mandatory for public companies and typically required for businesses seeking external financing. (See Part 2 for more details.)

EBITDA

EBITDA stands for earnings before interest, taxes, depreciation, and amortization. It is a metric used to evaluate a company's operating performance. Essentially, EBITDA measures profitability by focusing on earnings from core business operations, excluding the effect of financing options, tax environment, and noncash accounting items. This allows for a clearer comparison of performance across different companies and industries.

Fiscal Year

Unlike the traditional calendar year—beginning January 1 and ending December 31—a fiscal year is twelve consecutive months used by a business for financial reporting and budgeting purposes. A fiscal year can begin and end at any point in the year, but small businesses often choose to stick to the calendar year. You may consider several factors when determining your fiscal year, including the seasonality of your business, cash flow management, tax planning, and compliance requirements.

Fixed Costs

Also referred to as overhead, these are expenses that stay consistent, regardless of fluctuations in production or sales levels. These costs cover elements like rent, permanent employee salaries, software subscriptions, and insurance premiums. Since fixed costs are incurred regularly, they must be paid regardless of the level of business activity.

General Ledger

Each account in the COA has a corresponding general ledger, which serves as the main accounting record of a business. The general ledger systematically organizes and records all financial transactions, documenting every credit and debit entry in detail. This comprehensive, chronological record is pertinent for precise tracking of financial activities and preparing financial statements.

Gross vs. Net

Gross describes the total amount before deductions or subtractions, while *net* is the remaining amount after all relevant deductions, taxes, and other subtractions have been applied.

Journal Entries

Journal entries are used to record the details of financial transactions in your accounting software. (When bookkeeping was done by hand, records were written in the bookkeeping journal.) An entry includes the details of a transaction: date, accounts affected, and credit/debit amounts. Journal entries provide an audit trail and are the building blocks of a company's financial statements.

Month to Date (MTD)

This term refers to the period that starts at the beginning of the current month and extends up to the present day. MTD calculations may be used to track and compare performance, financial metrics, or other activities within the current month, assessing short-term trends and progress.

Noncash Expenses

These are expenses in a company's financial statements that do not involve an actual cash transaction. Noncash expenses represent adjustments for accounting purposes rather than actual cash payments. Examples are depreciation and amortization.

Primary and Non-primary Business Activities

Primary business activities (core operations) are the functions driving a company's main revenue stream, such as manufacturing, sales, and services. These activities directly relate to the company's primary purpose. Non-primary business activities, on the other hand, are supplementary functions that support the core operations but are not central to the company's main revenue generation, for example, investment income and gains from asset sales. While non-primary activities can contribute to overall profitability, they are secondary to the core business operations.

Profit and Loss Statement (P&L)

This financial statement, also known as an income statement, details a company's income, expenses, and profits over a specific period. It provides insights into the company's operational efficiency, profitability, and financial performance. (The components of the P&L will be covered in depth in Chapter 10.)

Profit Margin

Profit margin is the percentage of revenue that exceeds the costs, or how much profit a company makes for every dollar of sales. It indicates the overall profitability of a business and can be calculated for different levels: gross profit margin, operating profit margin, and net profit margin. (Chapter 10 will cover the specifics and provide examples.)

Reconciliation

Reconciling involves comparing financial records—typically bank statements to accounting ledgers—to confirm they are correct and agree. This process identifies discrepancies, ensuring that all transactions are properly recorded and accounted for.

Return on Investment (ROI)

ROI measures the profitability or efficiency of an investment by comparing the gain or loss relative to its cost. It is typically expressed as a percentage and calculated using this formula:

$$ROI = Net\ Profit\ /\ Investment\ Cost \times 100$$

This metric evaluates the effectiveness of a business's investments.

Variable Costs

Variable costs are expenses that change in direct relation to the level of production or sales activity. When production or sales increase, variable costs rise, and when production or sales decrease, they fall. These expenses are tied to the volume of goods or services produced or sold and may include material costs, hourly wages for workers, and sales commissions. Since variable costs fluctuate with business activity, they are a key factor that influences operational expenses and profitability.

Year to Date (YTD)

This term refers to the period that starts at the beginning of the current year and extends up to the present day. YTD calculations are commonly used in financial reports to compare current performance with previous periods, track progress toward annual goals, and evaluate overall trends and achievements within the year.

Interchangeable Accounting Terms

When pursuing financial literacy, it's important to recognize that different terms can often have the same meaning. These synonymous terms may be used interchangeably, depending on the context and specific accounting practices. Here are a few examples:

Revenue and *Sales*

Both terms refer to the income generated from normal business operations.

Net Income and *Profit*

Both terms indicate the amount of revenue that exceeds expenses. It's the final figure on a P&L after all costs, taxes, and expenses have been subtracted from the total revenue.

Fixed Assets and *Noncurrent Assets*

Both terms describe long-term operational assets that are not expected to be converted to cash within a year. Examples include buildings, machinery, and equipment.

Inventory and *Stock*

Both terms refer to the goods available for sale and the raw materials used to produce goods to sell.

Equity and Owner's Equity

Both terms refer to the amount of money that would be returned to shareholders if all of the company's assets were liquidated and all of its debts repaid.

Profit and Loss Statement (P&L) and Income Statement

Both terms refer to a financial report that summarizes the revenue, costs, and expenses incurred during a specific period.

Owner Investments/Contributions and Capital Contributions

Both terms refer to the funds and/or assets that business owners contribute to their company, either to start the business or to support its ongoing operations. These investments increase the owner's equity stake in the company. Depending on the business entity type, there may also be outside capital contributors (investors).

Chapter Highlights

- Understand the distinction between bookkeeping and accounting:

  - Bookkeeping—the recording of financial transactions like income and expenses

  - Accounting—the analysis and interpretation of financial data for insights and reports

- Businesses can choose between cash-basis and accrual accounting, each of which comes with distinct advantages and challenges.

- Accounting methods must be used consistently across accounting periods to ensure comparability and accuracy.

- Many accounting terms are interchangeable, such as *equity* and *owner's equity*, *inventory* and *stock*, and *income statement* and *P&L*.

Chapter Four

Financial Management Hierarchy

As an entrepreneur, you wear many hats and handle many responsibilities on your own. However, it's unrealistic to manage *everything* by yourself. You will sometimes need to bring in an expert or, at the very least, extra help. It's not unusual to be uncertain about the type of financial assistance your business requires, so let's go over the key roles to identify any gaps in your business's financial management.

The first thing to do is distinguish the different levels of financial operations. From there, you can determine the level of support required to keep your business financially healthy and thriving.

Financial administration *within* an organization involves three levels of professionals: the bookkeeper, the accountant, and the chief financial officer (CFO). You may also enlist support from tax professionals outside of your business. Each plays a unique role in gathering, managing, and reporting financial information, though the responsibilities often overlap. While your small business may not require this many individual people, ensuring that all functions are covered is imperative for maintaining business stability and compliance with regulatory requirements.

Level 1—The Bookkeeper

Level 1 in your financial management hierarchy is the bookkeeper. Bookkeeping, at its most basic, involves recording and categorizing transactions. (The basics of bookkeeping will be covered more in-depth in Part 2.) Bookkeepers are responsible for maintaining financial records, and they typically handle tasks such as running payroll, paying bills, sending invoices, making deposits, and maintaining ledgers. Their role is very task-driven and focused on data input. Basic knowledge of accounting principles and proficiency with your software program of choice are necessary if the bookkeeper is to record and organize financial data correctly.

Although you may not have an officially titled bookkeeper, someone must be tracking your business's financial data continuously. That *someone* may be *you*, but there are pros and cons involved.

If your company has no employees, handling the bookkeeping yourself can keep you in tune with your business's finances. Although keeping your own books may save you money in payroll, you must spend your valuable time learning how to do the books and then keeping them constantly up to date. Your time is worth money and never more so than when you are launching a small business. Thus, handling your own bookkeeping is not necessarily the most cost-effective use of your personal resources. As the leader of a company, your time may be better used on the things only you can do rather than logging the details of every financial transaction.

If you do decide to handle it yourself, it's vital that you do it correctly. A consultation with a professional can help you set up your initial system and processes. A qualified accountant should create your COA (chart of accounts), providing you with a strong foundation. Remember, DIY bookkeeping can lead to costly mistakes for small business owners when they don't know how to do it well.

Once you grow, hire employees, increase the volume of transactions, and can't keep up with the bookkeeping consistently on your own, it's time to hire a bookkeeper—either part-time or outsourced—to handle your financial records efficiently.

Hiring

If you're ready to hire an employee to handle your bookkeeping, consider someone who has other skills too. Many administrative assistants can also handle basic bookkeeping tasks, especially if they receive some training. If you aren't ready to hire an employee—even part-time—outsourcing may be best for you. Bookkeeping is relatively easy to outsource.

For a newly formed small business, a bookkeeper might be able to do it all in less than five hours per month. For more established small businesses, the bookkeeping workload could be as high as ten to twenty hours per month, or even more, depending on your business model.

Prices will vary depending on how complex your company is and how many transactions you have each month. Outsourcing allows you to use and pay for just the resources and services you need. Outsourcing firms and individuals offer different price structures; some charge a flat recurring monthly service fee while others will charge hourly.

Level 2—The Accountant

Level 2 in the financial management hierarchy is the accountant. Accountants take over where bookkeepers leave off, analyzing and interpreting financial data (covered in Part 3 of the book). This part of the financial process is often overlooked in small businesses, but it is crucial. Starting and running a company without accounting support is unwise.

An accountant will verify that your COA is set up correctly and prepare your financial reports: balance sheets, P&Ls, and cash flow statements. An accountant may also perform audits and provide advice for budgeting. They use financial information to determine the health of the company and provide business owners (and CFOs) with information to effectively strategize. Accountants often have more education and training in accounting principles than bookkeepers and may hold a bachelor's or master's degree in accounting or related fields.

Accounting work can also be outsourced. If you have someone in-house handling your bookkeeping (Level 1)—for example, an admin assistant—your accountant can check the bookkeeper's work for accuracy, be available for consultations, handle monthly reconciliations, perform journal entries for complex transactions, and provide advice.

If you already plan to outsource your bookkeeping, you might want to find an accountant who also handles bookkeeping. Ideally, this person would handle everything we discussed in Level 1, then be able to also cover Level 2: reconciling your books, providing finance reports, and being available to answer your questions. With an accountant's guidance, you can confidently understand your business's financial state and make informed, savvy decisions for the future.

Level 3—The CFO (Chief Financial Officer)

Level 3 in the financial management hierarchy is the chief financial officer. CFOs oversee the financial operations of a company. They are responsible for strategic planning and managing risks. CFOs analyze the company's financial strengths and weaknesses, propose corrective actions when needed, set pricing, decide on compensation levels, and track the financial health of the organization.

Most small business owners wear the CFO hat (in addition to all their other roles). If you can interpret financial reports and handle the responsibilities mentioned above, then you may be able to be your own CFO. This is not the case for many, though. If this isn't your strength, then you won't be able to go it alone. Running a business solo is hard, isolating, and challenging. You need a trusted, skilled person to interpret data, explain reports, guide strategy, lend an ear, and say the hard truths out loud.

If you require assistance, the solution is to hire a fractional CFO. A fractional CFO is an executive who provides high-level financial oversight and strategic planning services to businesses on a part-time or contract basis. This role is ideal for small companies in need of expert financial guidance but that cannot afford a full-time CFO (or do not have the volume of business to justify it). This person may bring experience from multiple industries, providing strategic financial planning, budgeting, and forecasting.

If you're on the fence about whether a fractional CFO is necessary, ask yourself these questions:

- Am I preparing and following through with my budget?

- Am I often unsure about my cash flow and how to optimize it?

- Am I looking to identify, assess, and mitigate financial risks more effectively?

- Am I seeking deeper insights into my financial data?

Who are you talking to about your company finances? Anyone? Having someone you can strategize with is advisable, and I strongly recommend consulting with a CFO.

To recap, let's review the three levels of financial operations:

- Level 1: The Bookkeeper—inputs data, records and categorizes transactions

- Level 2: The Accountant—confirms accuracy, analyzes and interprets financial information

- Level 3: The CFO—oversees financial operations, makes strategic decisions

Now that you know the details of each level, ask: Can I do any of this myself, or should I hire someone?

As mentioned earlier in the chapter, time is money, and business owners often find themselves stretched thin for time. Handling your financial operations can be challenging, especially with other pressing responsibilities. Unless you enjoy it and know how to do it well, you will likely want to offload this work to focus on building your business.

Is a separate person required for all three levels?

No, not at all. You can outsource to an accountant who will also do your bookkeeping. Just know that you'll pay accountant-level fees for the bookkeeping—and that's OK! Or you can hire a fractional CFO who will also serve as your accountant. Some fractional CFOs will even handle all three levels. Or you can handle the bookkeeping on your own—just be sure to do it properly—and hire an accountant/fractional CFO to review your books monthly, verify the bookkeeping is being done correctly, interpret financial reports with you, and assist you with strategy.

Outsourcing financial work, however, requires careful oversight. You can delegate the work, but you *cannot* delegate the ownership of responsibility for the financial status of your business. Also, recognize that these professionals are not magicians. If you do not supply them with the information required (transaction details, bank statements, loan documents, etc.), they will not be able to accurately keep your books up to date. Your books are only as good as the data you provide.

When hiring, be sure you use the right terminology. Don't create a job listing for a bookkeeper when you actually need someone who can analyze data, handle complex journal entries, and strategize with you. And don't look for an accountant when you really require advice from a tax expert.

The following are responsibilities you could list in a job description for each of the three levels:

Bookkeeper

- Record daily financial transactions, including sales, purchases, and expenses.

- Update financial records and ledgers.

- Maintain an electronic filing system for receipts, invoices, and bank statements.

- Prepare and process invoices.

Accountant

- Prepare and analyze financial statements—P&Ls, balance sheets, and cash flow statements—each month.

- Conduct financial audits and oversee regulatory compliance.

- Perform month-end (and year-end) adjusting entries and reconciliations.

- Develop and implement internal controls to safeguard financial data.

- Provide accurate financial data for budgeting and forecasting.

Fractional CFO

- Guide business owner on financial strategy, planning, and navigating risk for the company.

- Oversee financial operations and budget management.

- Develop financial policies and procedures to optimize financial operations.

- Coordinate with external tax professionals and handle internal tax planning and compliance.

Protect Your Company

Regardless of who you hire, you must protect your company. Allowing employees or outsourced contractors to access your company's financial information is a delicate decision. Yet, delegating responsibilities is essential for scaling your business.

As your company grows, trying to handle everything on your own becomes unsustainable. You can't micromanage every aspect and expect to maintain momentum. Balancing transparency and accountability with security and risk management is vital when assigning tasks to others. Here are key considerations:

Checks and Balances

Establishing checks and balances prevents one person from having complete control over the finances. The division of financial duties among different people greatly reduces the risk of errors and fraud. For instance, the person who approves expenses should not be the same person who processes payments.

Additionally, conducting regular internal audits protects your company by discovering discrepancies and ensuring compliance with financial policies, assuring integrity overall. At the bare minimum, learn how to generate financial reports in your software by yourself. Do not solely rely on a bookkeeper to do this. Exported reports can be manipulated. Your oversight and ability to run reports are critical to safeguarding your finances.

Security Measures

You should implement security measures to protect your financial information. Give each member their own login credentials to prevent security breaches and accountability issues caused by shared passwords. Use role-based access control (RBAC), which grants access only to those who require it to do their job.

No one should be gatekeeping the books from the business owner. I've seen some shocking situations in which business owners didn't have login access to their accounting software or know the passwords for online banking accounts. As the business owner, you should have a separate login and password and be listed as the primary user of your accounting software. You own the business—you own these accounts.

Now, on to taxes...

Tax Professionals

Every business should engage a tax professional for accurate and timely tax filing. These professionals include certified public accountants, enrolled agents, tax attorneys, and others experienced in tax preparation. Your chosen tax professional should be credentialed and possess expertise in tax preparation to ensure the accuracy and compliance of your income tax returns.

The three tax professionals that follow are the ones who commonly work with small businesses. All three are not required; just one will suffice.

CPA (Certified Public Accountant)

CPAs are licensed accounting professionals who have met specific educational and experiential requirements and have passed the Uniform CPA Examination (similar to an attorney passing the bar exam). CPAs focus on higher-level accounting work, notably auditing and preparing taxes. Not all accountants are CPAs. Notice the difference in the credentials and duties mentioned here compared to the previously described responsibilities of an accountant.

EA (Enrolled Agent)

EAs are federally licensed tax practitioners who specialize in tax preparation and have unlimited rights to represent taxpayers before the IRS. They have demonstrated their expertise in tax matters either by passing a comprehensive exam or through their experience as former IRS employees. EAs can handle tax issues, audits, appeals, and collections.

Tax Attorney

Tax attorneys can prepare and file your taxes, but they are more commonly sought out for their expertise in tax planning, resolving tax disputes, and providing legal advice on complex tax matters.

Can an accountant without these credentials file my taxes?

Yes, but it is not advisable. Small business owners must comply with financial regulations and tax laws, which can be complex and change frequently. Staying current with these regulations and ensuring compliance is challenging and time-consuming. When you hire a credentialed tax professional, you can be sure that they have the most up-to-date knowledge regarding taxes.

Do I only need a tax professional at tax time?

Tax season is, of course, the one time of year when you absolutely must work with a tax professional. However, I recommend you begin your relationship well before tax time, ideally when starting your business, by consulting a tax professional about your tax classification and business model.

Once you are up and running and with an accounting process in place, ask for a consultation to review the setup. This additional review will mitigate problems, uncover opportunities, keep the business in compliance with IRS regulations, and reduce the stress of tax time. Allow your tax professional the opportunity to be proactive when it comes to your finances instead of reactive once the year is over.

Also keep in mind that many small business owners should pay quarterly taxes, depending on your tax classification and other factors (additional income, tax obligations, etc.). This is another item to consult with your tax professional about.

Can my tax professional also do the other three levels of financial management?

Yes, a tax professional is more than qualified to handle the other levels of financial operations, but it is unusual to find one who is willing to do so. Some firms may offer all of these services as a package, but the work is spread among team members with different levels of expertise.

How to Choose a Tax Professional

Selecting the right tax professional is paramount. First, confirm their credentials. This can be done online with the corresponding issuer of their credential: the IRS for EAs and the State Board of Accountancy for CPAs.

But confirming credentials is the bare minimum. Beyond qualifications, consider the following:

- Experience and Specialization—look for professionals with experience in your industry and with businesses of your size and structure. They will have better insight into the unique tax issues and opportunities your business may face.

- Reputation—check online reviews and testimonials. Ask for references from other small business owners in your network.

- Services Offered—ensure the professional offers services beyond tax preparation, in particular tax planning, consulting, and audit representation. Verify that they can meet your specific needs (e.g., payroll taxes, sales taxes, international tax issues).

- Fees—ask about fees and billing structure. Do they charge a flat fee or an hourly rate? Request a clear estimate of costs up front, including any additional fees for extra services.

- Comfort Level—trust your instincts, and choose someone you feel comfortable discussing your financial matters with. Ensure that they respect confidentiality and handle your financial information securely.

- Availability—confirm they are available when needed, especially during tax season and at year-end. Consider their accessibility—whether they are easy to reach via phone, email, and/or in person.

- Communication Skills—assess their ability to explain tax concepts in a way you understand. This is a big issue. I've worked with countless clients who have a bad relationship with their tax professionals. The right professional will work *with* you and wants to see your company succeed. You should never feel dismissed or dumb after meeting with them. You shouldn't dread your interactions with them. (You can dread the amount of money you have to pay in taxes, but not the interaction with the person telling you that amount.)

Be cautious of tax preparers who display these red flags:

- Promise larger refunds than others

- Charge fees based on a percentage of your refund

- Suggest depositing your refund into their account, claiming it will then be sent to you

- Refuse to sign your return

- Ask you to sign a blank return

Questions to Ask When Vetting a Tax Professional

1. What are your qualifications and professional credentials?

2. How many years of experience do you have working with small businesses, specifically businesses in my industry?

3. Can you provide references from other small business clients?

4. What is your fee structure and what services are included?

5. How do you stay updated on the latest tax laws and regulations?

6. What happens if I'm audited? Will you interact with the IRS on my behalf?

7. What tax planning strategies do you recommend for small businesses in my industry?

8. What does your tax preparation process look like?

9. How often will we communicate, and how quickly do you respond to queries? What method of communication will we use?

10. How will you provide confidentiality and security of my financial information?

Choosing a reputable tax professional requires careful consideration. Taking the time to find the right fit can save you money, reduce stress, and support tax compliance. Download The Small Business Finances Toolbox for a full guide to choosing a tax professional.

Chapter Highlights

- Three Levels of Financial Management—each role has distinct responsibilities, but they often overlap.

  - Level 1—The Bookkeeper records and categorizes transactions, maintains financial records, processes payroll, and handles bills and invoices. Bookkeepers focus on data entry and must have basic accounting knowledge.

  - Level 2—The Accountant analyzes and interprets financial data, prepares reports, assists with budgeting, and ensures reliable financial records. They may handle more complex financial tasks and audits.

  - Level 3—The Chief Financial Officer oversees financial strategy, navigates risks, and makes high-level decisions. Small business owners often act as CFOs, but a fractional CFO can provide expertise on a part-time basis.

- DIY Bookkeeping—small business owners may start by handling their own bookkeeping, but it can be time-consuming and possibly not the most cost-effective solution. Professional setup and advice are recommended.

- Outsourcing—assess your skills and hire when needed. Utilize the sample job responsibilities when seeking to outsource any of the three levels of financial management.

- Tax Professionals—engage a professional for tax planning and filing. Choosing the right tax professional involves verifying credentials, experience, and compatibility.

Bookkeeping

Next, we'll dive into the details of bookkeeping.

Setting up a financial tracking system should be one of the first steps when establishing your business. The system you choose should be simple and intuitive, allowing you to easily keep up with your bookkeeping tasks while effectively tracking all the money flowing in and out of your business.

Everything in your bookkeeping is tied to your chart of accounts, or COA, which is the financial hub of your business—a structured framework for tracking and reporting all income, expenses, and resources. It is essentially a comprehensive list of all the accounts you use for categorizing financial transactions. But don't confuse the term *account* here with a bank or credit card account. In bookkeeping, *accounts* refer to specific categories used to organize financial transactions. For every financial activity, you will select the appropriate "account" from the COA to record it.

Setting up your COA is not a do-it-yourself task. Technical accounting knowledge is required to avoid errors, so hire a professional to set it up for you, even if you plan initially to be your own bookkeeper. This professionally created COA lays a solid groundwork for your business's accounting system.

If your COA is set up incorrectly, it can result in the following:

- misclassification of accounts, which distorts financial performance

- errors in financial statements, which may impact your taxes

- compliance issues

- difficulty tracking specific transactions or expenses

- poor financial administration of the business

Assigning transactions to the correct accounts ensures precise record-keeping and reliable financial statements. Within the main accounts (listed below), subcategories can be created for improved tracking. (This strategy will be discussed in the coming chapters.)

Every account on your COA will fall into one of these five main categories, each of which will be covered thoroughly in the following chapters:

1. Revenue—income earned by the business from its primary activities, including sales revenue and service fees

2. Expenses—costs incurred by the business to generate revenue, including salaries, rent, utilities, and supplies

3. Assets—resources owned by your business, including cash, accounts receivable, inventory, and property

4. Liabilities—your business's financial obligations, such as accounts payable, loans, and taxes

5. Equity—your ownership interest in the business, including capital contributions from you and retained earnings

The use of double-entry accounting requires that every transaction affects two of the above accounts from your COA—one with a debit entry and one with a corresponding credit entry. The main criterion is that total debits must equal total credits.

Double-entry accounting is a core function of most accounting software, ensuring that every transaction has both a debit and a credit. The software enforces this principle by preventing data entry unless both sides of the transaction are recorded. However, understanding the core concept of double-entry accounting and its effect on your COA is still beneficial.

The following chart provides a visualization of how debits and credits increase or decrease the different types of accounts:

Increased By	Chart of Accounts	Decreased By
Credit	Revenue	Debit
Debit	Expenses	Credit
Debit	Assets	Credit
Credit	Liabilities	Debit
Credit	Equity	Debit

The following chapters will provide answers to these questions:

- What is revenue, and how is it recorded on the P&L?

- How can tracking revenue subcategories help in evaluating business performance?

- What are the fundamental components of an invoice?

- How should accounts receivable be managed to promote timely payments?

- What are the differences between variable and fixed costs?

- What is cost of goods sold (COGS)?

- How is inventory accounted for in my bookkeeping?

- What is the fundamental accounting equation, and how is it involved in financial tracking?

- What are the different types of liabilities, and how do I account for them correctly?

- What are the components of the equity in my business?

- How do I pay employees and/or contractors?

- How do I pay myself as a business owner?

- What are the steps of the bookkeeping process that should be performed monthly?

Chapter Five

Revenue

Let's begin with the most motivating line item on the COA: revenue. This is the lifeblood of any business and the reason we venture into entrepreneurship in the first place.

Revenue represents the primary source of income for your business, shown in the top line on the P&L (profit and loss statement). This is the total amount of money generated from your core business operations. When funds flow into your company, they are categorized as revenue, loans, or equity. Among these, revenue is the only one recorded on your P&L, while loans and equity are detailed on your balance sheet.

You can create subcategories for your revenue to effectively monitor such details as locations, product lines, and more. By tracking these as subaccounts, you can distinguish the best-selling categories and pinpoint accounts with lower sales. This enables you to determine which products or services may require additional advertising or promotion and even assess if certain offerings should be discontinued.

Here are example revenue subaccounts for each of our three fictitious businesses:

Joe's Woodworking

- Bookcases

- Coffee Tables

- Custom Work

A&J's Boutique

- Basic Apparel

- Footwear

- Children's Clothing

- Seasonal Apparel and Accessories

The Marketing Group

- Content Creation

- SEO Services

- Social Media Management

Payment Methods

Now that you've established a method for tracking revenue, it's time to choose which payment methods you will accept. The options will depend on various factors unique to your business. Do you operate online or in person? Are you B2B or B2C? Do you sell high-ticket items or lower-priced products? These considerations will influence the best payment solutions for your business.

Here is a list of commonly accepted payment methods:

- Cash—traditional and simple and still prevalent for in-person transactions

- Checks—still used by some businesses, especially for larger amounts or B2B transactions

- Bank/Wire Transfers—direct transfers from your customer's bank account to yours; often used for larger transactions (may have fees attached, depending on the type of bank account)

- Credit and Debit Cards—widely used and convenient for customers; accepted via point-of-sale systems and online payment gateways

- Digital Wallets and Mobile Payments—digital wallets (e.g., PayPal, Venmo) and mobile payment services (e.g., Apple Pay, Google Wallet) offer easy, contactless, and secure online and mobile payment options (true at the time of this writing, however, may change in the future)

Keep in mind the fees associated with electronic payments. While processing fees aren't ideal, they are a necessary cost of doing business. Numerous online payment processing services cater to small businesses, and their fees vary widely. Shop around for the provider best suited to your needs. Some charge a flat fee per transaction plus a percentage, while others may reduce the flat fee if your transaction volume increases over time. Investing time to research the best option for your business structure can save you money in the long run.

Invoicing

Invoicing depends on the type of business you run. Some businesses, particularly those in B2B sectors like manufacturing and professional services, regularly use invoices, while others, such as retail shops and restaurants, typically don't because they require immediate payment. This distinction is influenced by your business model, industry standards, customer base, financial strategy, and risk tolerance. If invoicing isn't relevant to your operations, feel free to move on to the next section.

For those of you who do invoice, let's explore the key components.

Elements of an Invoice

The common elements of a business invoice include the following:

1. Header—contains your business name, logo, contact information, invoice number for reference, and the word *invoice* clear and prominent at the top

2. Customer Information—the name, address, and contact details of the client you are billing

3. Invoice Date—the date the invoice is issued

4. Payment Terms—clearly stated to indicate when payment is due, any early payment incentives, late payment penalties, and the payment methods that you accept (more on payment terms to come)

5. Itemized List of Products or Services—a detailed breakdown of the products sold or services rendered, if applicable, specifying quantity (or hours), unit price, and total cost

6. Subtotal—the sum of all line item amounts before taxes or additional fees

7. Taxes—any applicable taxes (most commonly a sales tax) along with the corresponding amount

8. Discounts—relative product or service discounts and their amounts

9. Total Amount Due—the grand total, including taxes and discounts

10. Notes/Additional Terms and Conditions—additional information, such as special instructions on how to pay, or relevant terms and conditions regarding refunds or warranties

Together, these elements comprise a detailed invoice, promoting clear billing practices and streamlining payment processing between your business and your customers. Your accounting software may provide templates that can be easily customized.

Sample Invoice

Logo

Invoice #41523

Business Name
Address
Phone Number
Email

Invoice Date 01/28/25
Due Date 02/27/25

Bill To: Customer Name
Customer Address

Services/Product	Qty	Total
Product #1 ($100 each)	2	$200
Product #2 ($25 each)	6	$150
Product #3 ($15 each)	12	$180

Payment Method Options:
Check or credit card

Note : Payment terms Net 30. Please make the payment by the specified due date to avoid late fees.

Subtotal	$530
Tax(5.5%)	$29.15
TOTAL	**$559.15**

Thank you for your business!

Website url

Payment Terms

Decide in advance what payment terms you will use when invoicing your clients. Here are the most common payment terms for small business invoicing:

- Net 30—customers are required to pay the invoice within thirty days of the invoice date.

- Net 60—customers have sixty days from the invoice date to complete payment.

- Due Upon Receipt—payment is expected immediately upon receipt of the invoice.

- 50/50 Payment—half of the payment is due up front, and the remaining balance is due upon completion or delivery of the goods or services.

- Installments—payments are spread out over multiple installments, with specific amounts due at predetermined intervals.

Interest charges or late fees may be applied if customers fail to adhere to the agreed-upon payment terms, but it depends on policies established in your terms and conditions or contracts. To avoid confusion or arguments later, inform customers up front about your rules for late payments and any extra charges they might face.

Now that you know the components of invoicing, develop a process for how invoices are created and when they are sent. This process can vary from business to business. For example, some companies will invoice the client once work is complete. Others may require a deposit before work begins. Sending invoices as soon as you generate a sale or complete a task is best practice. Set up a system so that invoicing won't be neglected or pushed to the nonurgent task pile.

Accounts Receivable

Accounts receivable (also referred to as A/R or AR) are the amounts that customers owe you. When you issue an invoice, the amount is recorded as "accounts receivable." This is an asset item listed on your balance sheet, representing money owed to your business. If your company invoices clients for products or services, it's imperative that you closely monitor these accounts to ensure timely payments and improve your company's liquidity.

To manage accounts receivable effectively, you must do the following:

- Send invoices promptly after delivering products or completing services.

- Offer multiple payment options to make it easy for customers to pay.

- Review open invoices weekly and send reminders to past-due customers.

- Implement a consistent collections process to recover outstanding balances.

What about incoming money not tied to the business operations?

Any income from non-primary business activities is considered "other income." The transactions most frequently found here are cash-back rewards from your business credit card. Other possibilities may include the sale of an asset and investment income. Your company may not have anything in this category. If you're uncertain whether a transaction should be classified as revenue or other income, consult with your tax professional.

Chapter Highlights

- Revenue—revenue is the money generated from primary business activities. It is recorded on the top line of the P&L, unlike loans and equity, which are on the balance sheet.

- Revenue Subaccounts—tracking revenue by subcategories (e.g., product lines, locations) highlights high and low performers, which guides promotion, advertising, and/or product phase-outs.

- Payment Methods—common payment methods include cash, checks, bank/wire transfers, credit/debit cards, and digital wallets/mobile payments. Choose payment methods based on your business type, and consider the associated processing fees.

- Invoicing Process—establish a consistent invoicing process, such as invoicing upon completion of work or requiring deposits.

- Accounts Receivable—monitor accounts receivable to track customer payments. Practice timely invoicing, offer multiple payment options, review overdue invoices regularly, and implement a collections process.

Chapter Six

Expenses

Selling your product or services and generating revenue is exciting, but it's important to balance your enthusiasm with the reality that running a business incurs costs. Expenses can accumulate quickly and become overwhelming for small businesses. But if you're diligent in managing your finances, you'll have a much better handle on things.

In this chapter, I'll guide you through the different types of expenditures and teach you which items to track to maintain solid financial records.

Variable Costs vs. Fixed Costs

Your company's expenses will consist of variable and fixed costs.

Variable costs are expenses that fluctuate in direct proportion to the level of production or sales. They fall when production decreases and rise when production increases. These costs vary with the volume of goods or services produced or sold and may include the cost of materials, wages of hourly workers, and sales commissions.

Fixed costs are expenses that stay consistent regardless of fluctuations in production or sales. These expenses commonly include rent, salaries of full-time staff, insurance premiums, software subscriptions, website hosting fees, and business license fees. Fixed costs are recurring in nature and require payment regardless of the business's revenue level.

Knowing how to distinguish between variable costs and fixed costs helps businesses analyze cost structure and gauge profitability. Variable costs directly relate to production levels and can be adjusted in the short term, while fixed costs remain steady over a specific period and require careful budgeting and planning.

Cost of Goods Sold (COGS)

Cost of goods sold (COGS)—also referred to as direct costs, cost of services, or cost of sales—is its own expense category listed separately from other expenses. While often associated with manufacturing businesses, COGS can also apply to retailers and service-based businesses.

Despite the word *goods* in the label, this accounting category can be used even without a physical product. COGS is a prime example of a variable cost, but it can include some fixed costs, depending on the business and type of expense.

Any direct costs involved in producing or acquiring the goods or services your company sells to its customers will be categorized as COGS. Included on the P&L, these costs are subtracted from revenue to determine gross profit. Accurately reporting COGS ensures that your financial statements correctly represent operational profitability.

For your bookkeeping, you can create subaccounts under COGS to track specific costs, such as direct labor, materials, freight, and subcontracted services. This detailed tracking contributes to better oversight of production expenses. Depending on your accounting software capabilities, you can track expenses (and income) directly related to specific jobs or projects. (See Chapter 10 for more details on COGS and how it is represented on your P&L.)

Here are examples of COGS subaccounts for each of the three businesses:

Joe's Woodworking

- Supplies and Materials—cost of raw materials and components used to create the final product (e.g., wood, nails, sandpaper, wood stain, and other materials)

- Labor—wages and salaries of employees *directly* involved in creating the product*

- Manufacturing Costs—costs related to production (e.g., equipment maintenance and depreciation of equipment)

* Do note that the owner of Joe's Woodworking will not receive wages or salary due to its being a sole proprietorship. (If you are a sole proprietor, see Chapter 8 for information about how to pay yourself.)

A&J's Boutique

- Products—cost of products purchased for resale, but only moved to this account once they are sold (see below*)

- Freight or Shipping Costs—expenses incurred to deliver the inventory to the shop

- Packaging—cost of shopping bags and price tags

* Inventory is considered an asset (not an expense) until it is *sold*. After the inventory is sold to a consumer, the costs associated with the inventory (whether purchased or manufactured) are considered COGS. (Chapter 7 will cover this in more detail.)

The Marketing Group

- Labor—"billable hours" directly tied to the service the client is paying for (e.g., consultation hours)

Operating Expenses

While direct costs (COGS) are deducted from revenue to calculate gross profit, operating expenses are the additional indirect costs required to run your business. Although both contribute to your operations, it's important to note that COGS and operating expenses are separate categories, and expenses cannot be counted in both. Operating expenses are not directly associated with a particular product or service and therefore are also known as indirect expenses, including such costs for advertising and marketing, administration, and distribution.

Operating expenses should be divided into well-defined accounts, and those accounts can be specified further into subaccounts. Which accounts and subaccounts you use is dependent on your type of business. It's recommended that you use different accounts and subaccounts when categorizing expenses for several reasons:

- Clarity and Organization—creating a clear and organized system for tracking your company's financial transactions makes it easier to analyze expense patterns, uncover cost-saving opportunities, and prepare reliable financial reports.

- Budgeting and Forecasting—providing insights into past spending patterns allows for anticipation of expenses and effective resource allocation.

- Tax Compliance—ensuring that expenses are properly recorded and classified according to tax regulations will mitigate the risk of errors, audits, and penalties related to tax reporting. Tax laws are ever-changing. Consult with your tax professional regarding the required expense categories to track and itemize.

Here are some of the more common operating expense accounts:

- **Advertising and Marketing**—expenses related to promoting your business and products or services (e.g., advertising campaigns, marketing materials, website development, and social media marketing)

- **Bank Fees and Charges**—costs incurred for various banking services provided by financial institutions (e.g., transaction, overdraft, wire, and ATM fees; account maintenance; etc.)

- **Dues and Subscriptions**—expenses related to memberships, subscriptions, and professional affiliations that support the operation or growth of the business (e.g., membership fees for industry associations, trade publications, and professional organizations)

- **Insurance**—premiums paid for various types of coverage (e.g., property, liability, workers' compensation, etc.) (Consult an insurance agent to determine which policies will best protect your business.)

- **Interest**—the cost incurred from borrowing funds or obtaining financing for the business (e.g., interest payments on loans, lines of credit, and other forms of debt used to support operations or growth initiatives)

- **Legal and Professional Services**—fees paid to external professionals (e.g., consultants, legal advisors, CPAs) for their expertise and services

- **Meals and Entertainment**—expenses for business-related dining, client entertainment, and staff social gatherings (e.g., client lunches/dinners, group meals, and entertainment functions aimed at networking, relationship-building, and business discussions)

- **Merchant Fees**—charges for processing credit and debit card transactions through a merchant account (i.e., imposed by payment processors or banks)

- **Office Supplies**—costs incurred by purchasing consumable items needed for daily office operations (e.g., paper, pens, printer ink, etc.)

- **Payroll**—costs associated with compensating employees for their work, including salaries, wages, bonuses, and benefits (health insurance, retirement contributions, etc.)

- **Rent/Lease**—the cost of renting or leasing office space, retail space, warehouses, or other facilities necessary for the operation of the business

- **Repairs and Maintenance**—expenses associated with repairing and maintaining equipment, machinery, and facilities used in the business operations

- **Software and Technology**—fees related to purchasing or licensing software, computer hardware, and other technology tools that support the operation of the business

- **Taxes**—various taxes levied on a business's income, property, or operations (e.g., income tax, property tax, sales tax, payroll taxes) (Additional information on taxes will be provided later in this chapter.)

- **Travel**—expenses incurred for business-related travel (e.g., transportation, hotel accommodations, etc.)

- **Utilities**—expenses related to essential services (e.g., electricity, water, gas, heating, telecommunications)

- **Vehicles**—costs associated with operating and maintaining company vehicles used for business purposes (e.g., fuel, maintenance and repairs, insurance, registration fees, depreciation)

These are just suggestions. Your business is unique and may require different categories. You may or may not require subaccounts within them. For example, if your business doesn't require a lot of software or technology, assigning all such expenses to the main category will likely suffice. But if your company is tech-heavy, it may be beneficial to track different types of software or technology into subaccounts. This will allow you to generate better data for improved analysis.

Depreciation and Amortization

Both depreciation and amortization are noncash expenses, meaning that no money changes hands. Instead, there is an accounting adjustment. These expenses allow for the allocation of the cost of assets over their useful lives. The process ensures a true representation of the assets' decreasing values and the corresponding expenses in a company's financial statements.

Depreciation

This applies to tangible assets: machinery, buildings, vehicles, furniture, and equipment.

Example: If you purchase machinery for $12,500 with a ten-year useful life, each year the machinery depreciates due to wear and tear. The first year's depreciation expense is recorded on the P&L, reducing the asset's book value on the balance sheet to $11,250. This reflects an annual depreciation expense of $1,250.

Amortization

This applies to intangible assets: patents, copyrights, trademarks, goodwill, and software.

Example: If you acquire a patent for $20,000 with a ten-year useful life, you amortize $2,000 annually. This expense is recorded on the P&L, reducing the patent's book value on the balance sheet to $18,000 after the first year. This process continues until the asset is fully amortized.

How to Calculate

The IRS provides specific rules for calculating depreciation and amortization, making it imperative that you consult with a tax professional to confirm compliance with accounting standards and tax regulations.

Why is it important?

- Financial Reporting: Recording depreciation and amortization provides a realistic picture of asset values.

- Tax Reporting: These expenses can offer tax benefits by allowing deductions over time.

- Asset Management: Tracking the reduction in asset values aids in making decisions about maintenance, repairs, and replacements.

Are all expense categories tax-deductible?

Not all categories listed on a P&L are tax-deductible. Whether an expense is tax-deductible depends on various factors, including the nature of the expense, the tax laws in the jurisdiction where the business operates, and how the expense is incurred. Generally, expenses that are ordinary and necessary for the operation of the business are tax-deductible, but you must consult with a tax professional or accountant to determine the deductibility of specific expenses based on the relevant tax regulations. For example, as of this writing, meals are only 50 percent deductible.

Contra Revenue

A contra revenue account is a special type of bookkeeping account used to represent reductions to revenue. These items are subtracted from the main revenue account on the P&L to calculate net revenue, as opposed to being recorded as an expense. You may sometimes see contra revenue accounts listed under COGS rather than in a separate contra revenue section on a P&L.

These are the three commonly used contra revenue accounts:

Returns

If a customer returns a product or you issue a refund for a service, the transaction should be categorized here.

Discounts Given

This category refers to reductions in the selling price, offered to customers as an incentive for various reasons. These discounts could be given for early payment, bulk purchases, promotional events, and other marketing reasons.

Allowances

This account is for products sold to customers at a reduced price due to the product being defective, damaged, and so on.

Sometimes these three expense accounts are lumped into one line item. If you have a high volume of these expenses, consider separating them to provide better tracking.

What about expenses not tied to the core business operations?

Expenses not tied to the core operations are infrequent, and you may not have any at all. Some examples include loss on the sale of an asset, a lawsuit settlement, or—depending on your type of business entity—federal income taxes.

Taxes

Navigating taxes can be complex and overwhelming, but it's critical that you not overlook them. Understanding your tax responsibilities and adhering to laws and regulations is imperative. Seeking guidance from a tax expert will optimize planning strategies to minimize liabilities and maximize benefits. While the cost of hiring a credentialed professional may be high, when it comes to taxes, it is a necessity.

Choose a professional who is accessible and willing to work closely with you to establish proper bookkeeping practices and offer valuable advice. Many small businesses engage tax professionals who simply "do" their taxes without offering strategic guidance. Instead, enlist a professional with expertise in serving small businesses and who specializes in your industry. (For tips on hiring the right tax professional for your needs, refer to Chapter 4.)

Small businesses have tax obligations that vary based on their business type. These obligations can differ significantly, especially across different states, and in certain cases even cities. What follows is a concise summary of the taxes you should be aware of and review with your tax advisor.

Income Taxes

Small businesses are subject to federal, state, and sometimes local income taxes on the profits they earn. The specific tax rates and filing requirements vary depending on the business's structure and jurisdiction. Most small businesses are pass-through entities, which means the tax obligation is passed through the business and on to the owners/shareholders. The following are pass-through entities:

- Sole Proprietors—pay income taxes personally on their IRS Form 1040

- Partners—use IRS Form K-1 to prepare personal income tax returns

- S Corporation Owners—receive a K-1 and pay the taxes personally (similar to partners)

Depending on earnings, most pass-through entities are required to make estimated federal income tax payments throughout the year to cover income and self-employment tax liabilities (see below). These estimated tax payments are made four times throughout the year and help businesses meet their tax obligations on time. Failure to do so can result in penalties.

Be aware that even though they are frequently referred to as "quarterly" tax payments, their deadlines do not equally break the year into three months.

- Q1: January 1–March 31 (three months)

- Q2: April 1–May 31 (two months)

- Q3: June 1–August 31 (three months)

- Q4: September 1–December 31 (four months)

This payment schedule refers to federal income taxes, but some states also require estimated quarterly taxes. How do you know if you should pay estimated taxes federally and/or on the state level? Consult with your tax professional.

C corporations are recognized as separate taxpaying entities (not pass-through). The company files an IRS Form 1120 and pays income tax on its profits. Shareholders are paid dividends and are personally responsible for paying income tax on them.

Self-Employment Taxes

As a business owner, you may be responsible for paying self-employment taxes. These taxes are calculated based on your net earnings, the business entity type, your salary (or lack thereof), and other variables.

Employment Taxes

If your business has employees, you must withhold federal and state income taxes, Social Security taxes, and Medicare taxes from their wages. Additionally, employers are responsible for paying a portion of Social Security and Medicare (FICA) taxes on behalf of their employees (more on this in Chapter 8).

Sales Taxes

Depending on what you sell and where, you may be required to collect and remit sales tax. Sales tax rates and regulations vary by state and locality. This is a pass-through tax—you collect it from the customer and then pass it on to the local governing agency. The only cost to you is the time and resources dedicated to the collection and remittance of the sales tax amount.

Property Taxes

You may be taxed on property your business owns: land, buildings, and other assets. These taxes are calculated based on the property's value and assessed by state and/or local governments.

Franchise Taxes

This tax is often described as paying for the privilege of operating a business. Franchise taxes vary significantly depending on your business entity and your location.

Excise Taxes

Certain businesses may be required to pay excise taxes on certain goods—such as alcohol, tobacco, and gasoline—services, or activities. The rates and requirements for these taxes are set by federal, state, and local governments and are often passed on to the customer (similar to sales tax).

Business License and Permit Fees

In addition to taxes, small businesses may be required to obtain business licenses or permits from local or state governments to operate legally. These licenses and permits often require payment of fees or taxes based on the type of business activity or industry.

Managing Employee Expenses

To promote accountability, establish and communicate clear financial policies to all employees, specifying guidelines on spending, reporting, and the use of company funds. Implement systems to hold employees accountable for their financial actions, for instance, maintaining detailed records of transactions and requiring approvals for large expenditures.

To best handle employee expenses, you will want to use expense reports. Expense reports offer detailed tracking and provide clear documentation of spending, allowing the business to retain control over approved expenses. Implement a solid process for how employees will complete and turn in their reports.

Also, consider the pros and cons of using expense reimbursement versus company cards to determine which method best fits your business needs and risk tolerance. Using a process in which the employee personally pays for expenses and applies to be reimbursed later can be appropriate for occasional expenses (when issuing a company card is not practical). However, this comes with an administrative burden, requiring time and effort to review and approve the reimbursement, manually enter the bookkeeping transaction, and process the reimbursement payment. In addition, employees must wait for reimbursements, which affects their personal cash flow. Some employees may not be able to carry this burden, and it's not ethical to force them to do so.

Example Expense Report				
Employee Name		January 2024		
Date	Merchant/Vendor	Category	Amount	Notes
12/4/24	Uber	Travel: Rideshare	$28.44	
12/4/24	Restaurant ABC	Travel: Meal	$23.98	
12/5/24	Restaurant 123	Meal: Client	$129.42	Meeting with Client XYZ
12/6/24	Hotel XYZ	Travel: Hotel	$493.87	
12/6/24	Uber	Travel: Rideshare	$27.11	

If you utilize expense reports and reimbursements, ensure that your bookkeeping is precise. These employee reimbursements are considered business expenses and *not* the employee's taxable income. Misclassification could result in inaccurate year-end tax documents for your employee.

Company cards provide convenience by giving your staff immediate access to company funds for business expenses, reducing the administrative burden of manual transaction entry. They offer control through spending limits and real-time transaction monitoring. Despite these advantages, there is a higher risk of unauthorized spending if the credit card is not closely monitored, and it requires diligent reconciliation of card statements with actual business expenses.

Regardless of how expenses are paid, keeping receipts and records is vital. Complacency or assumptions of trust can be dangerous for your company. Checks and balances are necessary to avoid fraud and embezzlement.

Chapter Highlights

- Variable vs. Fixed Costs—variable costs change with production levels (e.g., materials, hourly wages), while fixed costs remain constant regardless of production (e.g., rent, salaries).

- Cost of Goods Sold (COGS)—COGS includes direct costs associated with the production of goods or services and is a component of your gross profit calculation. It is separate from operating expenses.

- Operating Expenses—these are indirect costs required to run the business (e.g., advertising, bank fees, insurance, payroll, etc.). They should be categorized clearly for better budgeting, forecasting, and tax compliance.

- Tax Considerations—businesses must plan for various taxes (e.g., income, self-employment, sales, property). Understanding tax obligations and consulting with a tax professional is crucial for compliance and optimization.

- Expense Tracking and Oversight—establishing clear policies and systems for tracking employee expenses, handling reimbursements, and regulating company credit cards is important for maintaining financial control and accountability.

Chapter Seven

The Accounting Equation

Assets = Liabilities + Equity

Assets: what you own

Liabilities: what you owe

Equity: the difference between the two

The accounting equation demonstrates the fundamental principle of double-entry accounting. The double-entry method is what keeps the accounting equation balanced.

Debits are used to increase asset accounts. Credits, on the other hand, are used to increase liabilities and equity accounts. Here is the chart from earlier in the book for a visual reminder of debits and credits.

Increased By	Chart of Accounts	Decreased By
Credit	Revenue	Debit
Debit	Expenses	Credit
Debit	Assets	Credit
Credit	Liabilities	Debit
Credit	Equity	Debit

This equation is also the basis of your balance sheet. We'll delve into the specifics of that report and how these accounts balance one another in a later chapter. For now, we'll break down the three components of this equation.

Assets

Assets are items of value that your business owns or has rights to. This includes cash in the bank, inventory (products available for sale), equipment (e.g., computers or machinery), and money owed to you by customers (accounts receivable).

For some small businesses, their only asset is the money they have in the bank. Others may have a range of assets used to operate and generate revenue. These assets fall into two main categories: current assets and noncurrent (long-term) assets. Each of these categories contains more specific subcategories.

The following are among the most common assets found in small businesses, though it is not an exhaustive list:

Current Assets

Current assets are assets expected to be converted into cash or used within one year. Common types of current assets include the following:

- Cash and Cash Equivalents—include cash on hand and readily available funds in checking and savings accounts

- Accounts Receivable—amounts owed to the business by customers for goods sold or services rendered on credit; typically short-term assets that will convert into cash once the customers pay their invoices (Refer to Chapter 5 for more details on invoicing and managing your accounts receivable.)

- Inventory—goods or products that the business has for sale or use in the production process; may include raw materials, work-in-progress, and finished goods; considered an asset for businesses involved in manufacturing, retail, and wholesale operations

- Prepaid Expenses—payments made in advance for expenses that will be utilized in future accounting periods (e.g., prepaid insurance premiums, rent, subscriptions) (By recording prepaid expenses as assets, companies recognize their right to use these services or assets in the future, which will be gradually expensed over time as they are consumed or utilized.)

Noncurrent Assets

Also referred to as long-term assets, noncurrent assets are expected to provide economic benefits beyond one year. They are often further categorized into tangible and intangible assets. Common types of noncurrent assets include the following:

Tangible Assets

- Property, Plant, and Equipment (PP&E)—land, buildings, machinery, equipment, vehicles, and furniture used in the production or operation of your business; recorded at their original cost minus accumulated depreciation (more on depreciation later)

- Investments—long-term investments in securities, bonds, or equity of other companies held as part of a financial portfolio

- Long-Term Notes Receivable—amounts owed to the company by borrowers with due dates extending beyond one year

Intangible Assets

Assets that have value but no physical substance are called intangible. Intellectual property is an example—patents, trademarks, copyrights, and trade secrets—as well as goodwill and brand recognition. Intangible assets contribute to the competitive advantage and long-term success of a business but may require specialized evaluation methods. Seek professional advice when needed.

Assets contribute to the overall stability and value of small businesses. Proper management and valuation of these assets will maximize their benefits and support the long-term success of the business.

Now, we'll take a more thorough look at inventory, since it is one of the more complicated types of assets, requiring close oversight.

Inventory

Not all companies have inventory. But if your business model is retail or manufacturing, your inventory will significantly influence various aspects of your financial reporting.

Here are some common valuation methods for managing inventory:

- FIFO (First In, First Out)—this method operates on the premise that the first items placed into inventory are the first ones sold. This is the method most used by small businesses as it provides a more realistic valuation of ending inventory. It is used frequently by those who sell items with expiration dates; by selling the oldest inventory first, FIFO enables products to be sold before their quality degrades.

- LIFO (Last In, First Out)—this method assumes the most recently produced or purchased items are sold first. While less common for small businesses, LIFO may be advantageous for those who sell products prone to significant price fluctuations; during periods of rising costs, it results in a lower taxable income due to the higher expense.

- Weighted Average Cost (WAC)—this method calculates the average cost of all units available for sale. Small businesses may favor this simpler approach, especially small retailers that carry a large amount of low-cost, interchangeable items (e.g., office supplies, hardware, basic clothing). This method makes inventory tracking and valuation a more efficient process.

- Specific Identification—in this method, the actual cost of each item for sale is tracked. While more precise, many feel this inventory costing method is overly complex and time-consuming. Small businesses that sell unique, high-value items like antiques, fine art, or luxury goods may find the specific identification method best for their business.

Select the inventory valuation method best suited for your type of business, and stick to it. Inventory represents a significant portion of a company's assets, so accurately tracking and valuing it will allow you to produce more reliable financial statements. Misrepresenting inventory can distort your assets on the financial reports.

Inventory Cycle

When purchased, inventory is recorded at cost as an asset on the balance sheet, including additional expenses like freight (shipping to you) and handling fees. Inventory remains classified as an asset on the balance sheet until it is sold, when it is then reclassified as a business expense.

Periodic adjustments to your inventory counts should be part of your inventory cycle. The frequency of counts and adjustments will depend on your business model, either monthly, quarterly, or—the bare minimum—annually. Be consistent. Accurate inventory counts are necessary to maintain precise inventory records.

At the conclusion of your selected time frame, you will evaluate your inventory figures and proceed to make adjustments, which may include the following:

- Inventory Remaining (asset)

- Sales Revenue (income)

- COGS (expense)

- Shrinkage (expense)

Using your inventory valuation method, you will determine the value of your remaining inventory. The value of the inventory remaining at the end of the period is considered an asset on the balance sheet and is carried forward as the beginning inventory for the next period. The amount of inventory not carried forward to the next year should be moved to the appropriate expense accounts (COGS, shrinkage, etc.).

The sale of inventory generates revenue and, hopefully, profit. This revenue is recorded on the P&L. Concurrently, the cost of the inventory sold is recorded as COGS on the P&L. (Refer to Chapter 6 for more specifics about COGS.) Again, the value of the sold inventory is calculated according to your inventory valuation method.

If there is a discrepancy between the previous inventory numbers and what remains, it is considered shrinkage. Shrinkage could be the result of theft, damage, or inaccurate record-keeping and is listed as an expense on your P&L.

Proper inventory bookkeeping plays a vital role in maintaining financial control and regulatory compliance. Inventory levels directly affect tax calculations, as different valuation methods affect reported taxable income and liabilities. Well-documented inventory records are an integral component required to adhere to accounting standards. Diligently tracking inventory prevents discrepancies that could lead to audit issues or regulatory scrutiny. Inventory valuation confirms that your data truly reflects the business's financial state.

Here is an example of an inventory adjustment:

After an inventory count, A&J's Boutique needs to account for $1,425 worth of inventory that was sold and $75 worth that was damaged.

Account Name	Debit	Credit
Inventory		$1,500
Cost of Goods Sold	$1,425	
Shrinkage	$75	

The credit of $1,500 decreases the inventory asset, whereas the offsetting debits increase the expense accounts of COGS and shrinkage.

Liabilities

Since we've discussed your business assets, we'll now move on to the money your company owes. Liabilities are your debt. This may include loans you owe to the bank, bills you haven't yet paid, credit cards, and money you owe to suppliers.

Small businesses have a variety of liabilities. Similar to assets, they are divided into two overarching categories: current liabilities and noncurrent (long-term) liabilities. Under these general categories are more specific types.

Current Liabilities

Current liabilities are debt obligations expected to be paid within one year. Common types of current liabilities include the following:

- Accounts Payable—amounts owed to suppliers or vendors for goods or services purchased on credit

- Short-Term Loans—money borrowed or credit arrangements due to be repaid within one year (the most common being credit cards and lines of credit)

- Accrued Expenses—expenses incurred but not yet paid (e.g., wages, utilities, and taxes payable)

- Unearned Revenue—payments received from customers for goods or services but not yet delivered or provided

Noncurrent Liabilities

Also referred to as long-term liabilities, noncurrent liabilities are obligations *not* expected to be paid within one year. Common types of noncurrent liabilities include the following:

- Long-Term Loans—money borrowed or credit arrangements due to be repaid over a period longer than one year, including mortgages

- Deferred Tax Liabilities—tax obligations payable in future accounting periods due to temporary differences between accounting and tax rules

- Leases—commitments for property, equipment, and vehicles extending beyond one year, showing the company's obligation to make payments over the lease term

- Owner Loans—funds lent to the business by the owner(s) and not expected to be repaid within the next year

These are just a few types of small business liabilities. Most small businesses incur liabilities to access capital and boost cash flow, and each has its own benefits and considerations.

Depending on the type of business you have (or plan to start), initial capital may be required to cover a variety of startup costs, for example, purchasing equipment, securing a physical location, developing products or services, and marketing to potential customers. If you're just starting a small side hustle without a lot of overhead costs, funding may not be needed, or you may use your personal savings to cover the expenses. But for many entrepreneurs, the startup costs are more than they have in their personal bank accounts.

Let's dig into the details of a few types of debts and loans and their potential bearing on your company's financial situation.

Accounts Payable

Accounts payable (also referred to as A/P or AP) is the category that includes the funds your business is obligated to pay suppliers or vendors for goods, inventory purchases, and services obtained on credit. It generally includes unpaid invoices or bills from suppliers or vendors.

Managing accounts payable involves more than just paying bills; it encompasses a range of tasks that enable smooth financial operations, such as meticulously tracking supplier invoices, strategically scheduling payments to optimize cash flow and avoid late fees, and reconciling accounts to identify discrepancies. To avoid damaging relationships, pay your suppliers and vendors on time. Consistently falling behind on accounts payable can be detrimental to your business's health and should be remedied immediately.

Credit Card Debt

Credit cards are somewhat necessary for operating a business. The benefits are numerous: They make business purchases easy and convenient, and many offer cash-back perks and travel rewards. If you provide your employees with a credit card, you can easily control how much they spend and have immediate oversight of their purchases.

However—if at all possible—pay your credit card balance *in full* each month. Avoid carrying credit card debt, which typically has high interest rates that can quickly accumulate and become unmanageable. I've seen it happen countless times. You may have a couple of big purchases one month and say, "I'll get caught up and pay it off next month." Then it repeats and repeats, resulting in a debt snowball that is challenging to get under control.

Instead, look to borrow money through loans with more favorable terms and lower interest rates. These loans can provide more predictable and manageable repayment schedules, reducing financial strain and improving long-term financial stability. A little research and leg work can save you a significant amount of money in interest expense.

Loans

Securing a loan from a bank, credit union, the Small Business Administration (SBA), or an alternative lender (possibly a friend or family member) can provide the funds to launch your business and establish a strong foundation for future growth, without the significantly high interest rates of a credit card.

Borrowing money for startup costs comes with its own set of considerations. On the one hand, obtaining a loan can allow you to take advantage of early opportunities and grow your business faster than relying solely on personal savings. On the other hand, taking on debt means committing to regular repayments, which will affect cash flow and financial stability in the early stages of your business.

It is crucial to carefully determine your borrowing needs, understand the terms and conditions of the loans, and develop a solid repayment plan you can stick to. Keeping your credit—business and personal—in good standing should be a top priority. This will allow for easier borrowing in the future.

The most suitable loan type for your business will depend on the financing amount, your creditworthiness, and the purpose of the loan. Look for loans with low fees and interest rates, such as term loans, lines of credit, SBA loans, and microloans.

Personal Loans

If you have personal money to contribute to your company, you can do so in one of two ways. One is owner contribution, which is considered equity and not a liability. (Details to come in the next section of this chapter.)

The second way you can inject money into your business is through a personal loan—meaning you personally loan money to your business. For small businesses, this kind of loan is often used to finance long-term investments and cover cash flow shortages.

If you choose to go this route, you must treat it as you would a legitimate third-party loan. This means creating a formal agreement/promissory note, with these details:

- Full Loan Amount/Principal

- Payment Terms

- Interest Rate

Once the loan agreement is established, you will record it in your bookkeeping as you would any other third-party loan, adhere to the repayment schedule, and pay yourself consistently.

How Loans Impact Your Bookkeeping

Once you secure a loan, it should be listed on your balance sheet as a liability. Each monthly payment made will affect two items in your COA. First is the portion of your payment that goes toward the principal balance. (The principal is the total amount you borrowed.) A payment toward the principal will decrease the liability amount on your balance sheet. The second item impacted is the interest expense (or finance charges). With each loan payment, the interest amount should be recorded as an expense on your P&L. At the end of the year, verify the interest expense is recorded and confirm that the remaining principal balance is accurate.

Equity

Your company's equity represents the health of your business. It is what remains after you subtract liabilities from your assets. If you had to liquidate your business today, you would sell your assets to pay off liabilities. The remainder is what you would walk away with, and that is considered your equity.

Equity in a small business includes contributions and distributions by owners/shareholders.

Contributions and Distributions

Contributions are the initial capital investments made by the owner(s) as well as any additional contributions made over time. This is different from a personal loan made to a business (see the previous section about loans). No promissory note is attached to this money nor interest fees paid to the owner(s).

Distributions are withdrawals made by the owner(s).

For sole proprietorships and partnerships, these are referred to as "owner contributions" and "owner distributions." For partnerships, there will be multiple owner accounts. These should be listed individually by name to track what each owner has contributed or withdrawn.

For corporations (S or C corps), an owner is referred to as a shareholder. Therefore, on the balance sheet, these line items are labeled "shareholder investments" and "shareholder distributions."

There are other nuanced elements involved in the equity for corporations: common stock, preferred stock, undistributed earnings, and more. As mentioned in an earlier chapter, a business must meet multiple requirements before being eligible to become a corporation. Once your company meets those requirements, you must work closely with a tax professional to comply with regulations regarding shareholder equity. You should not attempt to handle this on your own. (We'll cover additional details about equity and how it's displayed in your financial reports in Chapter 11.)

Chapter Highlights

- Fundamental Accounting Equation—the accounting equation is Assets = Liabilities + Equity, which indicates the balance of a company's bookkeeping.

- Double-Entry Accounting—every transaction will be recorded in two accounts (categories) and involves a debit and a credit, ensuring total debits equal total credits to keep the equation balanced.

- Asset Categories—assets are divided into current (e.g., cash, accounts receivable, inventory) and noncurrent (e.g., property, equipment, intangible assets).

- Inventory Controls—inventory is an asset that can be valued using methods like FIFO, LIFO, weighted average cost, and specific identification, each of which affects financial statements differently. Once sold, the cost of inventory moves from an asset to COGS on the P&L.

- Liabilities—liabilities are categorized into current (e.g., accounts payable, short-term loans) and noncurrent (e.g., long-term loans, deferred tax liabilities), representing what the company owes.

- Consequences of Loans—loans are recorded as liabilities on the balance sheet, and repayments affect both the principal balance and interest expense lines on your COA.

- Equity—equity represents the value of assets that remains after deducting liabilities. It includes owner contributions and distributions (for sole proprietorships/partnerships) or shareholder investments and distributions (for corporations).

Chapter Eight

Paying Your Team and Yourself

Although payroll is commonly viewed as an expense, it can also affect other categories in your COA, including liabilities and equity. Due to its complexity, payroll gets its own chapter.

Initially, many small businesses operate with one owner and no staff. However, depending on the nature of your business, you may soon require additional support, whether through contract workers or employees. If you are considering expanding your team and wish to establish an efficient hiring process, consider reading *The Hiring Process*, a book from *The Team Solution Series*, which I co-authored.

Hiring employees and setting up payroll is tedious, and the process involves laws and regulations you must adhere to. Hiring starts with paperwork, much of which will be federally and state-required forms. These include I-9, W-4, and other tax forms possibly required by your state. Work with your tax and legal professionals for federal and local labor compliance. In the United States, refer to the Department of Labor, or DOL (dol.gov), for additional information. If outside the United States, be sure to follow the governing regulations in your area. Compliance is critical.

Salary vs. Hourly Employees

When building your team, differentiate between salary and hourly employees for budgeting and operational efficiency. Here's a brief overview of the distinctions and their financial significance:

Salary Employees

- Paid a fixed annual amount, regardless of hours worked

- Generally receive consistent paychecks, which aids in budgeting and business stability

- Often (but not always) exempt from overtime pay requirements

- Typically receive benefits (e.g., health insurance, paid time off, retirement plans), increasing your overall compensation costs

Hourly Employees:

- Paid according to the number of hours worked, which allows you to adjust your labor costs based on demand

- Fluctuating wages, which impact payroll predictability

- Eligible for overtime pay (usually time and a half) for hours worked beyond the standard forty-hour workweek

- May not receive the same level of benefits as salaried employees

Independent Contractors

Instead of hiring employees, you may choose to contract out the work. Contractors can be paid a fixed fee or project-based payment for completing specific projects or deliverables. The payment amount is agreed upon in advance and may be paid in installments or upon project completion. Some contractors charge an hourly rate for their services. They submit invoices for the hours worked, and payment is made based on the agreed-upon rate.

Unlike employees, contractors are responsible for paying all the taxes associated with their compensation, including income and self-employment taxes, as businesses are not required to withhold taxes from their payments. Additionally, contractors are not entitled to employee benefits (e.g., health insurance, retirement plans, paid time off).

Ramifications of Misclassification

It's vital to grasp the legal and regulatory requirements for paying contractors versus employees and salary versus hourly employees. Consulting a legal or HR professional will facilitate compliance and risk mitigation.

If an employer incorrectly classifies an employee as salaried when they should be hourly, several issues can arise:

- Unpaid Overtime—the employer may owe the employee back pay for overtime worked. Hourly employees are entitled to overtime pay under the Fair Labor Standards Act.

- Back Taxes—the employer may owe back taxes for the above unpaid overtime.

- Legal Penalties—the employer could face fines and penalties from the DOL for violating wage and hour laws.

- Lawsuits—the employee may file a lawsuit against the employer for unpaid wages, including overtime.

- Loss of Trust—misclassification can damage the relationship between employer and employee, leading to a loss of trust and potentially higher employee turnover.

Incorrectly categorizing someone as an outside contractor when they actually function as an employee can trigger several repercussions:

- Back Taxes and Penalties—the employer may be liable for unpaid employment taxes (e.g., Social Security and Medicare taxes, unemployment insurance, and other payroll taxes). They may also face penalties and interest on top of these amounts.

- Legal Action—the misclassified worker can file a complaint with the DOL or take legal action against the employer. The DOL may also independently investigate and impose fines.

- Benefits and Protections—the employer may be required to provide back pay for unpaid overtime, minimum wage violations, and benefits employees are entitled to by law.

- State Consequences—each state has its own penalties and enforcement regulations. Employers could face additional state-level fines and back taxes.

- Reputational Damage—misclassification can damage the company's reputation, making it harder to attract and retain talent.

This is just a brief overview of the repercussions that could arise from misclassification. To avoid serious financial, legal, and operational consequences that could devastate your business, you must carefully evaluate the nature of your working relationships and classify workers based on IRS and other relevant criteria. This is why working with a legal professional who specializes in employment and labor laws is a must.

Payroll Frequency

Once you decide to hire employees, determine how frequently you will pay them: weekly, biweekly, semimonthly, or monthly. Recognize how the frequency will affect your cash flow and administrative workload. The following lists some pros and cons of each frequency:

Weekly
(Example: every Friday)

Pros:

- Possibly improved morale and retention because employees appreciate being paid more frequently

- Helps employees manage their personal cash flow better

- Easier to track hours worked

Cons:

- Increased administrative workload due to more frequent processing

- Higher payroll processing costs

- Greater impact on cash flow, requiring consistent cash availability

Biweekly
(Example: every other Friday)

Pros:

- Balances employee preference for frequent pay with lower administrative burden (compared to weekly and monthly)

- More manageable payroll processing costs than weekly

- Simplifies budget forecasting with regular, predictable pay periods

Cons:

- Slightly more complex compared to monthly, especially for salaried employees

- Still requires relatively frequent cash availability

Semimonthly
(Example: 1st and 15th of each month)

Pros:

- Aligns more closely with monthly financial obligations for both the business and employees

- Reduces administrative tasks compared to weekly or biweekly

- Consistent pay dates make budgeting easier

Cons:

- Can be confusing for employees due to the varying number of workdays in each pay period

- May require adjustments for months with holidays or fewer workdays

- Mid-month pay periods might disrupt cash flow management

Monthly
(Example: 1st of each month)

Pros:

- Minimizes administrative workload and payroll processing costs

- Simplifies budgeting and financial planning for the business

- Reduces frequency of cash flow disruptions

Cons:

- Possibly difficult for employees to navigate personal finances with less frequent pay

- Increased risk of employee dissatisfaction and/or turnover due to longer intervals between paychecks

- Longer timeline before any payroll errors can be fixed

When choosing a payroll frequency, consider your business's cash flow stability and administrative capacity as well as the financial well-being of your employees. Balancing these factors will guide you to the optimal payroll schedule for your organization.

Performance-based Pay

In addition to salary and hourly compensation, you may choose to pay your employees based on performance. Performance-based pay can come in a few different forms.

Commissions

Commission is compensation tied directly to sales performance. It is typically calculated either as a percentage of the revenue generated from sales or a fixed amount per sale. Commission structures can vary widely, from straight commission (in which earnings are solely based on sales) to base salary plus commission.

Sales Performance Incentive Funds (SPIFFs)

This is a specialized bonus program aimed at rewarding specific behaviors or achievements beyond regular commission earnings. It's utilized as a temporary incentive to enhance performance over a short period, focusing on specific products or objectives. The incentive can be either monetary or non-monetary rewards.

Bonuses

A bonus is an additional compensation beyond regular salary or hourly wage, often based on overall company performance or individual achievements. Bonuses can be issued to reward exceptional performance, achievement of predetermined goals, or milestones met—going above and beyond expected job duties. They can be one-time or recurring, typically awarded annually or at specified intervals.

While all three—commissions, SPIFFs, and bonuses—are used to incentivize employees, they serve distinct purposes in aligning employee actions with business objectives, rewarding performance, and driving results at different levels and time frames. Work with a professional who can advise you about their differences and how they are reported as employee income. For example, the IRS currently considers bonuses to be supplemental income that is taxed differently than regular wages. Again, tax and labor laws are ever-changing. Consulting with an expert will help you comply with all regulations.

Employment Taxes

When it comes to having employees, employment taxes are a necessary burden. Some taxes are withheld from the employee's paycheck, and you pass that amount on to the appropriate entity. Other taxes are the employer's burden and are paid by you.

These are the various taxes deducted from employees' paychecks:

- Federal Withholding Taxes—these taxes are withheld from the employee's income and paid to the IRS. The amount withheld is determined by the employee's wage amount, marital status, and number of exemptions (dependents).

- Social Security and Medicare—both of these taxes are remitted to the IRS, but they are calculated individually and at varying rates. There are annual limits, and the rates can fluctuate, underscoring the importance of staying informed about the current figures. Both taxes are withheld from the employee's earnings and matched by the employer, qualifying them as "fringe benefits" for employees. The combined total is paid to the IRS.

- State Withholding Taxes—each state has its own income tax rates (and several states have no state income tax). You can find information about the withholding rates for state income taxes from your state's Department of Taxation.

- Local Withholding Taxes—the city or town where your business operates may impose a tax that must be withheld from your employees' paychecks and paid to the local authorities.

Keep in mind that if you hire remote employees who live in different locations, you need to account for varying state and local tax withholdings. Employees may reside in areas with local wage taxes that you are responsible for withholding and paying on their behalf.

Some employment taxes are not withheld from the employee's wages but rather are paid by you, the employer. These taxes are the employer's burden:

- Federal Unemployment Tax (FUTA)—calculated quarterly, FUTA must be paid to the IRS once the amount exceeds a specified threshold.

- State Unemployment Tax (SUTA)—paid quarterly to your state's tax authority, this tax applies to an employee's wages up to a state-specific limit, which can vary.

- Workers' Compensation Insurance—while not a tax, this insurance fund covers workplace injuries. Some states allow businesses to self-insure. Employers contribute a percentage of each employee's wages, based on their job classification. Be sure to review your state's regulations for specific details.

Employee Benefits

Providing employee benefits is optional but worth consideration for the sake of remaining competitive with other employers and drawing top talent to your business. Determine what you can feasibly provide. Here is a brief overview of some benefit options you may consider offering:

- Medical Insurance

- Dental Insurance

- 401(k) Retirement Plans

- Health Savings Accounts

- Group Life Insurance

- Disability Insurance

Remember that employees can contribute toward these benefits. For instance, you could provide health insurance as a benefit, covering a portion of the monthly cost, while the employee covers the remainder.

Outsourcing Payroll

Calculating, tracking, and paying all of the above may sound overwhelming. When it comes to payroll administration, you can choose to handle it internally or opt to outsource. Although there is a fee associated with outsourcing, the advantages are substantial:

- Time Savings—outsourcing payroll frees up time your business can allocate to core activities like strategy, sales, and customer service, rather than spending hours on complex payroll tasks.

- Accuracy and Compliance—payroll providers are experts in payroll processing, tax laws, and regulations, reducing the risk of costly penalties and errors.

- Cost Efficiency—outsourcing can be more cost-effective than handling payroll in-house, especially for small businesses. It eliminates the need for specialized payroll staff and reduces expenses associated with payroll software and systems.

- Security and Confidentiality—payroll processing involves sensitive information. Outsourcing to a reputable provider supports secure data management by using advanced technology and processes to protect against data breaches and fraud.

- Access to Expertise and Technology—payroll providers offer the latest technology and software solutions, along with expert knowledge. This allows businesses to benefit from advanced payroll capabilities without having to invest in expensive systems and training.

There are numerous options for outsourcing this work—from your CPA firm to online software and a myriad of choices in between. I highly recommend you consider outsourcing payroll. The payroll provider will make sure your tax payments are correct and timely and that employees are sent accurate W-2s and contractors 1099s before the deadlines.

How do I pay myself?

As a small business owner, you have some options for paying yourself, which depend on your business structure, financial situation, and personal preferences. Let's go over the most common methods.

Owner's Draw or Distribution

In sole proprietorships and partnerships, you can withdraw funds directly from the business account for personal use. Keep in mind that this method does not involve withholding for taxes and payroll deductions. Also, this withdrawal is not considered an expense on your P&L. It is taken from your equity on the balance sheet.

If you have previously made personal contributions to the company, you can withdraw that amount from the company (as long as you have the cash flow to cover it). Beyond that, you can also withdraw as much as your company has made in net income (or retained earnings from previous years).

Guaranteed Payments

Applicable only to partnerships, guaranteed payments are a fixed payment amount that partners agree to receive, regardless of the business's profitability. Unlike owner distributions, these payments are treated as operating expenses for the business, but taxes are not withheld as they would be for employees. The amounts for these payments are specified in the partnership's operating agreement and must be disbursed even if the company is not profitable. Therefore, it's essential to carefully evaluate whether your small business can sustain these payments with its cash flow. Additionally, there are legal considerations surrounding guaranteed payments, so it's advisable to consult your tax professional.

Salary or Wages

If your business is a corporation (S or C corp), you can receive regular income as an employee through payroll, with taxes withheld the same as other employees. But the wages you pay yourself must pass the IRS's reasonable compensation test. (Again, consult with a professional for your specific situation.)

Dividends

If your business is structured as a corporation, you can also receive income in the form of dividends. Keep in mind that dividends are subject to other taxation.

For owner compensation, establish a clear payment method, maintain precise financial records, and seek guidance from a tax professional to align with your unique circumstances, tax obligations, and financial objectives. Compliance with legal and regulatory standards regarding payroll, taxes, and corporate governance should be a priority.

Chapter Highlights

- Regulatory Compliance—hiring involves various forms and compliance with federal, state, and local laws. Adherence to labor regulations is critical.

- Employee Classification—differences between salary and hourly employees, as well as between employees and independent contractors, affect budgeting, cash flow, and legal compliance.

- Payroll Frequency—deciding how often to pay employees (weekly, biweekly, semimonthly, or monthly) affects cash flow, administrative workload, and employee satisfaction.

- Performance-based Pay—commissions, SPIFFs, and bonuses can incentivize employees and align their goals with business objectives.

- Employment Taxes—employers are responsible for various taxes, including federal and state unemployment taxes, Social Security, and Medicare. Proper administration and payment are imperative.

- Owner Compensation—the method used to pay yourself as the business owner will vary depending on your business structure.

Chapter Nine

The Bookkeeping Process

As the previous chapters covered the individual aspects of bookkeeping, it's now time to bring everything together and review the complete bookkeeping process. Whether you handle it yourself or outsource it, you'll find in this chapter the steps to follow. I recommend completing this process every month for optimal financial management.

Input Data

The first step in the bookkeeping process is data collection. All financial transactions should be promptly and accurately entered into your accounting software. These transactions include all those that occur in your bank and credit card accounts.

Automating this process by syncing with your financial accounts or uploading statements directly into the system is highly recommended. While manual entry is possible, it increases the risk of errors, especially as transaction volumes grow. Automated bookkeeping not only reduces mistakes but also improves efficiency, allowing you to focus on strategic business priorities rather than routine data entry.

Categorize Transactions

Every transaction must be categorized appropriately based on your COA, which includes expenses, revenue, assets, liabilities, and equity, as discussed in previous chapters. This task can be done daily, weekly, or at least monthly, depending on the volume of transactions. The higher the volume, the more frequently you should complete this step.

Tip: Many accounting software programs offer automation features that can auto-categorize recurring transactions, boosting efficiency.

If you're uncertain about how to categorize a transaction, some accounting software includes an "ask my accountant" category in the COA. If this feature isn't available, you can create a placeholder account for uncertain transactions. This prevents transactions from being lost or misclassified and allows for later review with your tax professional. While this feature is helpful, it should be used sparingly. If you find yourself frequently using this category, it may be time to consult with a financial expert to avoid ongoing confusion.

Make Adjustments

Once all data is input and each transaction categorized, it's time to make adjustments before proceeding with the month-end reconciliation. These adjustments encompass a range of scenarios and are recorded as journal entries at the end of an accounting period—typically monthly or annually—to ensure the financial statements represent the company's financial position and performance.

What follows are a few common situations when it is necessary to record adjustments to your books.

Accrual Accounting

In accrual-based accounting, adjusting entries ensures that income, expense, asset, and liability accounts accurately reflect all transactions that have occurred but have not yet been recorded. This process aligns with the accrual basis of accounting, in which income and expenses are recorded when earned or incurred, regardless of when cash is received or paid. It is necessary for maintaining the accuracy of the business's financial statements.

For this accounting method, the adjusting entries may impact these categories:

- Accrued Expenses

- Accrued Revenue

- Prepaid Expenses

- Unearned Revenue

For example, The Marketing Group receives a $2,000 down payment on a contract before work begins. Initially, this deposit was categorized as "consulting revenue." However, by the end of the month, no work had been completed, meaning the payment should be recognized as unearned revenue. An adjusting entry is then made to transfer the amount from consulting revenue (a revenue account) to unearned revenue (a liability account).

Account Name	Debit	Credit
Consulting Revenue	$2,000	
Unearned Revenue		$2,000

Adjustments can be made for businesses with cash-basis accounting as well. This is often seen with revenue deposits. Two common adjustments for small businesses, regardless of cash or accrual method, are for sales tax and merchant fees. While this can be done with each individual deposit, it is often more efficient to adjust these deposit entries every month. I will provide two examples.

Sales Tax

Joe's Woodworking collects a sales tax on items sold. Before the adjusting entry, the entire deposit amount (paid for by the customer with either cash or check) was recorded as sales revenue. However, a portion of the deposit was sales tax, collected to be paid to the state and/or county.

In this example, Joe has deposited $21,200 in sales revenue. The local sales tax rate is 6 percent. Therefore, $1,200 of the money deposited should be adjusted to the sales tax payable account (a liability) in his bookkeeping. The adjusting entry below shows a decrease in sales revenue and an increase in sales tax payable:

Account Name	Debit	Credit
Sales Revenue	$1,200	
Sales Tax Payable		$1,200

Merchant Fees

Many small businesses accept credit cards as payment and, as a result, incur fees for processing these credit card transactions. Recording the merchant fee is one of the most overlooked tasks I've seen in small business bookkeeping.

For example, A&J Boutique accepts both cash and credit cards in the store. The funds collected via credit card are deposited into the A&J bank account weekly. At the end of the month, they show deposits totaling $47,144.50. But those deposits do not reflect the gross revenue because the merchant fees were already deducted.

Refer to your merchant account statement to see the total amount in fees deducted. For this example, the fees were $942.89 for the month. Therefore, the actual gross sales amount was $48,087.39. The adjusting entry records a credit in revenue and a debit in the merchant fee expense account, which increases the value of each on the P&L.

Account Name	Debit	Credit
Sales Revenue		$942.89
Merchant Fees	$942.89	

Annual Adjustments

While some adjustments are made on a recurring monthly basis, others are more appropriately recorded during the annual close process at the end of the fiscal year. These latter adjusting entries are related to inventory and depreciation/amortization.

For businesses with inventory, a physical inventory count is often conducted at year-end to reconcile the recorded inventory balance with the actual stock. Inventory adjustments will involve the following items from your COA:

- Inventory Remaining (asset)

- Sales Revenue (income)

- COGS (expense)

- Shrinkage (expense)

(Refer to Chapter 7 for more details on navigating inventory.)

The calculation and recording of depreciation and amortization expenses for long-lived assets is also done as part of the year-end close. Given the potential complexities and nuances involved, consult your tax professionals to confirm that these annual adjustments are done in compliance with relevant accounting standards and tax regulations. (Refer to Chapter 6 for more information on depreciation and amortization.)

Reconcile

After recording and categorizing all transactions and then entering adjusting entries, the next step is to reconcile your bank and credit card accounts, a process often referred to as "balancing the books." Reconciliation involves comparing your business's bank and credit card statements with the general ledger to verify that all recorded transactions match. This step is required to maintain accuracy before generating financial reports.

Confirm that the ending balances in your bank and credit card statements align with the ending balances in your bookkeeping ledgers. Don't forget to reconcile other financial accounts, such as PayPal, as well. Any discrepancies between recorded transactions and actual account balances—possibly caused by missing transactions or recording errors—must be identified and fixed to ensure the reliability of your financial records. If the accounts don't balance, carefully review your statement and ledger to locate and rectify the discrepancy. Continue investigating and correcting until your ledgers match the bank statements exactly.

Regular and consistent reconciliation prevents cascading errors, which may lead to last-minute scrambles during tax season. Monthly reconciliation fosters financial transparency, security, and stability within your organization. Additionally, it plays a critical role in fraud prevention by detecting unauthorized transactions or fraudulent activity, allowing you to take prompt action to address security concerns.

Once you've completed these steps, the bookkeeping process for the month is finalized, ensuring that your financial reports are reliable and up to date. This sets the stage for reviewing and analyzing your financial data, which we'll explore in the next chapter.

Refine When Needed

As your business evolves, keep your COA up to date to accurately reflect your financial activities. Even after the initial setup, adjustments may be beneficial to accommodate changes in your operations.

Here are some examples of such changes:

Joe's Woodworking has sold directly to the customer but now has an opportunity to sell some items wholesale to a local store. Adding an additional revenue account to the COA will allow the tracking of these new sales.

A&J's Boutique currently only sells apparel, but the owners have decided to expand and also sell home decor. To see if this new product offering is profitable, an update to the COA should be made. Possible additions would be home decor subaccounts for the following:

- Revenue

- Inventory

- COGS

When The Marketing Group first launched, tech and software costs were minimal. However, as the team grew and became comprised of a primarily remote workforce, the "software and technology" category in the books became a substantial monthly expense. Setting up subaccounts for specific types of tech or software expenses will improve expense tracking. Some examples of subaccounts might include the following:

- Website/Hosting

- Hardware

- Software Licenses

- IT Services

Staying on top of these updates ensures that your financial reporting remains relevant and useful.

What if my books are a mess and not up to date?

The above process is ideal for when starting a business. All data is input regularly, categorizations occur consistently, and the books are reconciled monthly. This is an accountant's dream—but it's not always reality. There is a good chance you're reading this book after starting your business, and you've either attempted DIY bookkeeping or you've outsourced it to someone who over-promised and under-delivered. This is an incredibly common situation—one that the majority of my clients have been in when they hired me. This type of cleanup requires a meticulous eye and patience.

Here's a step-by-step approach to fixing and cleaning up messy and inaccurate bookkeeping:

1. Assess the Situation—take a comprehensive look at the current state of your books. Identify areas where errors, inconsistencies, or discrepancies exist. When was the last reconciliation? Have adjustments been made to prior-reconciled transactions?

2. Standardize the Chart of Accounts—review your COA, and confirm it is properly structured and organized. Standardize account names and categories to improve consistency and clarity in financial reporting.

3. Organize Financial Documents—gather all bank and credit card statements, loan documents, and other financial records. Organize them chronologically and categorize them by type. This will make it easier to discover missing or duplicated transactions and reconcile accounts.

4. Review Transactions—for transactions that have been questionably categorized, review to verify the correct classification.

5. Catch up on Backlog—if not all transactions have been entered into your books, catch up. Work methodically through the backlog. I recommend starting with the oldest transactions and working forward to the most recent.

6. Reconcile Bank and Credit Card Accounts—now that your data has been updated, reconcile your bank and credit card accounts with your bookkeeping records to confirm they match. Investigate and resolve discrepancies.

7. Implement Proper Controls—establish internal controls and procedures to prevent future errors and maintain reliable books. This may include segregating duties, requiring approvals for certain transactions, and conducting regular reviews of financial records.

8. Seek Professional Guidance—still feel like you're in over your head? You may encounter complex accounting issues or feel unsure about how to proceed. This is the time to secure professional help.

What if it's almost tax time and I have done nothing?

If you find yourself in this situation, trust me, you're not the only one. This isn't uncommon for very small businesses that are just getting started—especially for side hustles with minimal transactions.

First, before attempting to do it yourself, consider your time frame and deadline. It may be quicker and more efficient to hire a professional to clean up your books. They will have the expertise and tools to quickly organize your financial records.

For this situation, you will perform the bookkeeping process steps covered earlier, but I advise you not to tackle the entire year at once. Start one month at a time. Do not move on to the next month until the previous one is finalized and reconciled. This methodical approach will make the task less overwhelming.

You may realize that you are so far behind that you have to file for a tax extension. This happens more often than you might think, and it's nothing to lose sleep over. But don't let the extension lull you into complacency. Start immediately by getting your books caught up, even while the extension is in place. The last thing you want is to be in the same emergency a few months down the line.

The keys are not to panic and tackle it step by step. Hiring a professional can save you time and headaches. And be sure to stay on top of your bookkeeping going forward so you are not in this predicament again next tax season.

Chapter Highlights

- Input Data—start the bookkeeping process by entering all financial transactions into your accounting software. Electronically pulling the data from your bank is preferred to reduce errors and increase efficiency.

- Categorize Transactions—classify transactions into appropriate categories from your COA: expenses, revenue, assets, liabilities, and equity. Utilize automation tools when possible, and use a placeholder category for uncertain transactions.

- Make Adjustments—adjust entries to ensure accurate financial statements, including accruals for expenses and revenue and corrections for sales tax and merchant fees. Annual adjustments may include inventory and amortization/depreciation.

- Reconcile Accounts—reconcile bank and credit card statements with your general ledger to verify accuracy each month. Address discrepancies promptly to maintain financial transparency and prevent errors.

- Organize Chaotic Records—when faced with messy or outdated books, evaluate the condition, establish a consistent COA, arrange documents, scrutinize transactions, clear the backlog, and reconcile accounts. Consider consulting a professional.

- Tax-Time Prep—if you're behind on bookkeeping as tax season approaches, consider hiring a professional. Tackle one month at a time, and if necessary, file for a tax extension while continuing to get your books in order.

Accounting

In earlier chapters, we explored the individual components forming the foundation of your bookkeeping. Now we'll shift our focus to how these elements come together to generate the financial reports that will guide your business strategy.

Keep in mind that bookkeeping isn't just about preparing for tax season; these reports are powerful tools that enable informed decision-making. The best business decisions come from clear, reliable data. You can't grow or improve your business without knowing what's working and what isn't. Before generating the financial reports, confirm that your accounts are reconciled to guarantee reliable information.

As a small business owner, you probably have numerous questions like these that you're unsure how to answer:

- Is my business sustainable?

- Can I afford to hire someone?

- How much can I pay myself?

- Can I increase marketing efforts?

- How quickly can I pay off loans?

- What investments can I make in the company (e.g., software, equipment, employee benefits)?

The answers to these vital financial questions influence both your short-term and long-term business strategies. Scheduling time each month to review your financial reports and address these inquiries is a practice that can significantly boost your success.

The upcoming chapters will focus on the following items for each type of financial report:

- Components of the Report

- How to Verify Accuracy

- Strategies for Analysis

Chapter Ten

Profit and Loss Statement

We'll start with the report utilized the most: the profit and loss statement (P&L), also known as the income sheet or income statement. This is likely the report you are most familiar with. At its very basic level, the P&L details how much money your company has earned (profits) and spent (losses) for a time frame with a specific start and end date. The time frame may be this month, last quarter, year-to-date, or any other beginning and ending calendar dates.

This report may be a simplified version, highlighting only the main income and expense categories, or a more detailed report, which includes all subaccounts as outlined in Chapters 5 and 6.

Let's go over the typical elements found on a P&L, listed in the order they should appear.

Revenue

This is the top line of the P&L and is referred to as income, sales, or revenue. It may be displayed as one lump sum in a line item, or if tracking subaccounts, you can view revenue by sales category, location, product line, and so on.

Cost of Goods Sold (COGS)

As discussed in detail in Chapter 6, COGS are the direct costs involved in producing or acquiring the goods or services your company sells to its customers. This line does *not* include operating expenses.

Gross Profit

The gross profit line on your P&L represents the difference between your revenue and COGS. It shows how much money is made from core business operations, *after* deducting the direct costs associated with producing or acquiring those goods or services but *before* deducting other indirect/overhead expenses.

Revenue – COGS = Gross Profit

Operating Expenses

Refer to Chapter 6 for detailed information about what your operating expenses entail. Do remember that this line does not include owner distributions and/or payments to a loan principal (but it does include interest expenses).

Net Operating Income

Net operating income represents the profitability of your company's core business operations. The figure is calculated by subtracting operating expenses from gross profit. This excludes non-operating income and expenses (see "Other Income and Expenses"). This metric measures the efficiency and performance of operations, helping you understand how effectively the business generates profits from its core activities.

Gross Profit – Operating Expenses = Net Operating Income

Other Income and Expenses

The next section of the P&L is "other income and expenses." Not all company P&Ls will include this section. It includes any secondary activities such as investment income, cash-back/credit-card rewards, federal taxes, sales of assets, and other non-primary business activities.

Net Profit (or Loss)

This is the bottom line, both literally and figuratively, in business discussions, representing the ultimate financial outcome from business operations. It's the final line on the P&L, revealing what remains after deducting all expenses from revenue. A positive result indicates a profit, while a negative result represents a loss, indicating whether expenses exceed the revenue earned or not.

Revenue – COGS – Operating Expenses + Other Income – Other Expenses = Net Profit (or Loss)

Key Items to Verify Accuracy

Before analyzing your P&L (or any financial report), it's essential that you thoroughly review the validity of the information. It's not enough to simply glance at the numbers. Analyzing a report with unreliable data is a waste of time. What follows are the steps you should take to verify the accuracy of your P&L.

Start by closely scrutinizing your revenue figures:

- Review revenue transactions to identify any loans or investments mistakenly recorded as income.

- Confirm that all income sources are precisely recorded and properly categorized, ensuring that no revenue is missed or duplicated.

Next, look at COGS:

- Verify that this figure is correctly calculated to reveal the true cost of production.

- Check that COGS only includes direct costs associated with producing goods or services.

Then examine your expense items:

- Look for anomalies or unexpected fluctuations that may require further investigation.

- Ensure that the operating expenses are appropriately categorized, up to date, and assigned to the correct accounts to avoid misclassification that could distort financial analysis and reporting.

- Confirm that your loan principal payments are not listed as expenses (only the interest and finance charges are considered expenses).

- Review owner distributions to ensure they are not listed as expenses.

By taking the time to thoroughly review and validate the information on your P&L, you can confidently trust the reliability of this financial document. This, in turn, will enable you to effectively strategize, driving the growth and success of your business.

Analysis Strategies

Now that you know your statement is error-free, it's time to analyze it. As a small business owner, reviewing your P&L will provide insight into your company's financial health and reveal growth opportunities.

Here are the areas you should inspect, as well as questions to ask yourself:

Revenue

- Are there fluctuations to note with sales income?

- Are there opportunities to increase sales in certain product or service areas?

- Should I consider price adjustments to boost profitability?

- Which are my top-performing products or services, and how can I sustain or even propel growth?

- Which areas are underperforming, and should I rectify the situation or cut those offerings?

COGS

- Are my direct costs to produce or deliver my products in line with industry benchmarks?

- Can I discover ways to optimize these expenses?

Expenses

- Am I ensuring that every dollar is being put to good use?

- Can I identify unnecessary or redundant costs that can be reduced or eliminated?

- Are my recurring subscriptions and memberships still providing value?

- Is it time to shop around for more cost-effective alternatives?

- Can I scrutinize our overhead costs and reduce expenses without affecting my business operations?

Net Income

- If net income is lower than expected or negative, what are the specific components (of revenue and expenses) contributing to this? Are there areas in which I can implement adjustments to improve profitability?

- Is the net income sufficient to cover debt obligations, capital expenditures, and other financial commitments?

- How does the net income compare to my goals and/or industry benchmarks?

- Are there nonrecurring or one-time items included in the net income figure that may not be representative of the company's ongoing performance?

Ultimately, your net income figure is indicative of the profitability and overall financial well-being of your small business. It is your bottom line—the actual amount of money you have available to spend, save, or invest. Don't just glance at your net income; really dive in, recognize what it's telling you, and use that knowledge to drive your business forward.

Integrating your P&L into your financial review process drives growth and profitability. Here's why:

- Assessing Financial Performance—your P&L offers valuable insights into your company's health over specific periods: monthly, quarterly, or annually. By analyzing this report, you can determine whether your business is generating profits or incurring losses, which impacts pricing strategies, cost control, and investment opportunities.

- Strategic Planning and Budgeting—the P&L allows you to project future revenue, expenses, and profits based on historical data and market trends. This empowers you to set realistic financial goals, develop detailed budgets, and allocate resources effectively. (We'll cover the specifics of budgeting in Chapter 15.)

- Building Stakeholder Confidence—a strong P&L is pivotal for maintaining positive relationships with investors, lenders, and other stakeholders. It instills confidence and assists with securing financing and investments for business operations and expansion.

- Ensuring Tax Compliance—your P&L is an indispensable tool for tax reporting. The financial data it provides is required for preparing accurate tax returns and keeping your business in good standing with regulatory authorities.

Here is an example P&L for each of the three businesses using a different timeframe for each.

Joe's Woodworking
P&L Statement Cash Basis
Jan 1, 2024 to Dec 31, 2024

Income	
Revenue (direct sales)	
Bookcases	$38,750.77
Coffee tables	$55,892.55
Custom work	$125,178.10
Total revenue (direct sales)	$219,821.42
Wholesale revenue	$25,977.24
Total income	**$245,798.66**
Cost of goods sold	
Depreciation of equipment	$1,900.00
Equipment maintenance	$2,890.07
Labor	$40,000.00
Supplies & materials	$64,722.68
Total cost of goods sold	**$109,512.75**
Gross profit	**$136,285.91**
Expenses	
Advertising & marketing	$3,485.00
Bank fees & service charges	$85.00
Business licenses & registration	$590.00
General business expenses	$392.11
Insurance	$6,500.00
Interest paid	$1,284.93
Legal & accounting services	
Accounting fees	$1,750.00
Legal fees	$890.00
Total legal & accounting services	$2,640.00
Office expenses	
Office supplies	$2,306.22
Small tools and equipment	$1,578.45
Tech & software	$576.81
Total office expenses	$4,461.48
Payroll processing fee	$540.00
Taxes paid	
Sales tax paid	$12,287.42
Payroll taxes—employer paid	$3,825.85
Property tax	$1,875.92
Total taxes paid	$17,989.19
Utilities	$3,781.60
Total expenses	**$41,749.31**
Net operating income	**$94,536.60**
Other income	
Credit card rewards	$150.00
Interest earned	$48.29
Total other income	$198.29
Net other income	**$198.29**
Net income	**$94,734.89**

A&J's Boutique
P&L Statement Cash Basis
Oct 1, 2024 to Dec 31, 2024

Income	
Sales revenue	
Basic apparel	$45,336.21
Footwear	$30,883.28
Children's clothing	$18,967.33
Seasonal apparel and accessories	$28,744.22
Home decor	$14,322.78
Total sales revenue	$138,253.82
Returns and allowances	-$1,184.65
Total income	**$137,069.17**
Cost of goods sold	
Products & inventory sold	$54,220.55
Freight & shipping	$87.00
Shopping bags & price tags	$122.69
Total cost of goods sold	**$54,430.24**
Gross profit	**$82,638.93**
Expenses	
Advertising & marketing	$1,355.00
Business licenses & registration	$55.00
General business expenses	
Bank fees & service charges	$55.00
Uniforms	$267.93
Total general business expenses	$322.93
Insurance	$175.00
Interest paid	$151.18
Legal & accounting services	$454.00
Meals	$177.33
Merchant fees	$3,218.06
Office expenses	
Office supplies	$211.91
Tech & software	$725.13
Total office expenses	$937.04
Payroll expenses	
Payroll processing fees	$226.00
Wages	$16,805.28
Total payroll expenses	$17,031.28
Rent	$6,000.00
Shrinkage	$75.00
Taxes paid	
Sales tax paid	$3,472.94
Payroll taxes—employer paid	$1,597.16
Total taxes paid	$5,070.10
Utilities	$338.74
Total expenses	**$35,360.66**
Net operating income	**$47,278.27**
Other income	
Credit card rewards	$57.48
Interest earned	$14.46
Total other income	$71.94
Net other income	**$71.94**
Net income	**$47,350.21**

The Marketing Group
P&L Statement Accrual
Dec 1, 2024 to Dec 31, 2024

Income	
Services	
Consulting revenue	$48,500.00
Content creation	$31,000.00
SEO services	$13,750.00
Social media management	$11,950.00
Total services	$105,200.00
Total income	**$105,200.00**
Cost of services	
Billable hours	$12,000.00
Total cost of services	**$12,000.00**
Gross profit	**$93,200.00**
Expenses	
Advertising & marketing	$2,500.00
Contract labor	$2,375.00
General business expenses	
Bank fees & service charges	$75.00
Continuing education	$330.00
Memberships & subscriptions	$128.00
Total general business expenses	$533.00
Insurance	$250.00
Legal & accounting services	
Accounting fees	$500.00
Legal fees	$489.00
Total legal & accounting services	$989.00
Meals	$328.45
Merchant fees	$5,938.95
Office expenses	
Office supplies	$78.25
Shipping & postage	$12.83
Total office expenses	$91.08
Payroll expenses	
Benefits	$2,749.55
Payroll processing fees	$128.00
Wages	$53,834.62
Total payroll expenses	$56,712.17
Rent	$680.00
Software & technology	
Hardware	$345.16
IT services	$475.00
Software licenses	$593.25
Website & hosting	$84.28
Total software & technology	$1,497.69
Supplies	$79.23
Taxes paid	$6,983.82
Travel	
Airfare	$639.25
Hotels	$506.25
Meals	$239.79
Taxis & shared rides	$74.21
Tolls & parking	$25.00
Total travel	$1,484.50
Utilities	$349.37
Total expenses	**$80,792.26**
Net operating income	**$12,407.74**
Other income	
Credit card rewards	$85.39
Interest earned	$35.62
Total other income	$121.01
Total other income	**$121.01**
Net income	**$12,528.75**

Job Costing

Depending on the type of work your business does, tracking job costs may be beneficial. In this context, a "job" is a specific project completed for an individual client. Job costing is an accounting practice that involves tracking the costs associated with a specific project to calculate its profit or loss. Some accounting software makes this easier by offering features that let you tag each transaction associated with a specific job, allowing you to generate reports for that job.

Job costing serves as a smaller-scale version of the P&L, providing detailed data on the financial performance of a specific project. By recording the revenue earned from a job and subtracting the direct costs, you can gain valuable insights into the profitability of individual projects.

Some businesses will include overhead costs to get a full picture of each job's true expense, ensuring they account for indirect costs like utilities, rent, or administrative expenses. Others exclude overhead in job costing, focusing only on direct labor and materials for simpler or more immediate cost tracking.

By distinguishing which projects generate the highest profits, you can allocate resources more effectively and make better choices about future endeavors. This will aid you in pricing your products or services, identifying areas for potential cost-saving measures, and ultimately improving the overall profitability of the organization. While this level of revenue and expense tracking requires more time and attention, the results will empower you to optimize for greater success.

Joe's Woodworking

Job Costing

Jan 1, 2024 to Dec 31, 2024

Project income	
Custom work for Morgan	$21,750.00
Total project income	**$21,750.00**
Cost of goods for project	
Labor	$2,375.00
Wood	$10,328.00
Stain	$721.26
Misc supplies	$263.82
Total cost of goods for project	**$13,688.08**
Project profit	**$8,061.92**

Comparative Analysis

While reviewing your P&L for a single time period is beneficial, you can gain deeper insights into your company's financial health by conducting a comparative analysis. For instance, how does the net income of the current period stack up against previous periods? Examining these fluctuations can reveal whether net income is rising, falling, or staying consistent over time. By viewing the P&L in a comparative context, you can identify both positive and negative trends.

Let's look at some comparison reports you can utilize in your business strategy.

Current Month vs. Year-to-Date (YTD)

Including a YTD column on your P&L provides an accumulated total for the current year up to the present date. This feature offers several benefits:

- Current Month Performance—the YTD column compares your company's performance this month to previous months, allowing you to determine immediate needs and adjust accordingly.

- Snapshot of YTD Performance—a snapshot provides a quick overview of your performance for the year, enabling you to gauge whether the company is on track to meet its annual goals and objectives.

- Context for Current Month—by viewing the current month's performance within the larger context of year-to-date results, you can better evaluate how each month contributes to overall success. This aids in recognizing patterns, such as seasonal fluctuations, and in making adjustments to resource allocation.

Overall, comparing your current month to YTD enhances your ability to monitor financial health and ensure your short-term actions align with long-term goals.

The Marketing Group
P&L Statement Accrual
Month to Year Comparison

	December 2024	YTD 2024
Income		
Services		
Consulting revenue	$48,500.00	$573,500.00
Content creation	$31,000.00	$384,000.00
SEO services	$13,750.00	$175,250.00
Social media management	$11,950.00	$138,200.00
Total services	$105,200.00	$1,270,950.00
Total income	**$105,200.00**	**$1,270,950.00**
Cost of services		
Billable hours	$12,000.00	$158,000.00
Total cost of services	**$12,000.00**	**$158,000.00**
Gross profit	**$93,200.00**	**$1,112,950.00**
Expenses		
Advertising & marketing	$2,500.00	$34,000.00
Contract labor	$2,375.00	$37,880.00
General business expenses		
Bank fees & service charges	$75.00	$825.00
Continuing education	$330.00	$923.82
Memberships & subscriptions	$128.00	$725.00
Total general business expenses	$533.00	$2,473.82
Insurance	$250.00	$3,450.00
Legal & accounting services		
Accounting fees	$500.00	$8,350.00
Legal fees	$489.00	$2,358.00
Total legal & accounting services	$989.00	$10,708.00
Meals	$328.45	$4,593.72
Merchant fees	$5,938.95	$74,028.51
Office expenses		
Office supplies	$78.25	$1,198.35
Shipping & postage	$12.83	$78.21
Total office expenses	$91.08	$1,276.56
Payroll expenses		
Benefits	$2,749.55	$1,387.00
Payroll processing fees	$128.00	$589,325.95
Wages	$53,834.62	$26,401.29
Total payroll expenses	$56,712.17	$617,114.24
Rent	$680.00	$8,160.00
Software & technology		
Hardware	$345.16	$13,482.40
IT services	$475.00	$5,983.11
Software licenses	$593.25	$6,519.44
Website & hosting	$84.28	$4,750.00
Total software & technology	$1,497.69	$30,734.95
Supplies	$79.23	$782.39
Taxes paid	$6,983.82	$77,462.42
Travel		
Airfare	$639.25	$4,781.66
Hotels	$506.25	$5,771.33
Meals	$239.79	$2,127.90
Taxis & shared rides	$74.21	$804.62
Tolls & parking	$25.00	$250.00
Total travel	$1,484.50	$13,735.51
Utilities	$349.37	$3,987.22
Total expenses	**$80,792.26**	**$920,387.34**
Net operating income	**$12,407.74**	**$192,562.66**
Other income		
Credit card rewards	$85.39	$984.31
Interest earned	$35.62	$374.98
Total other income	$121.01	$1,359.29
Total other income	**$121.01**	**$1,359.29**
Net income	**$12,528.75**	**$193,921.95**

Date Comparison

A date comparison for your P&L is similar to YTD comparisons but involves evaluating equal time frames. This can be done on a period-to-period basis (e.g., monthly, quarterly) or year-to-year. Here are two examples:

- A report comparing Q3 to Q4 identifies short-term trends and seasonal effects.

- A comparison of this year's Q4 and last year's Q4 considers seasonal variations and provides data to compare the same season.

These comparisons offer you valuable insights into company stability, growth measurement, and the impact of business strategies, allowing for strategic adjustments to enhance profitability and efficiency.

A&J's Boutique

P&L Statement Cash Basis

Quarter Comparison

	Q3 2024	Q4 2024	Q4 2023
Income			
Sales revenue			
Basic apparel	$30,184.94	$45,336.21	$41,612.44
Footwear	$21,266.02	$30,883.28	$27,372.34
Children's clothing	$9,073.55	$18,967.33	$15,768.33
Seasonal apparel and accessories	$14,083.51	$28,744.22	$21,863.44
Home decor	$2,794.58	$14,322.78	$0.00
Total sales revenue	$77,402.60	$138,253.82	$106,616.55
Returns and allowances	-$634.85	-$1,184.65	-$963.44
Total income	**$76,767.75**	**$137,069.17**	**$105,653.11**
Cost of goods sold			
Products & inventory sold	$30,723.54	$54,220.55	$44,935.22
Freight & shipping	$65.00	$87.00	$95.00
Shopping bags & price tags	$89.23	$122.69	$99.40
Total cost of goods sold	**$30,877.77**	**$54,430.24**	**$45,129.62**
Gross profit	**$45,889.98**	**$82,638.93**	**$60,523.49**
Expenses			
Advertising & marketing	$975.00	$1,355.00	$1,115.00
Business licenses & registration	$0.00	$55.00	$55.00
General business expenses			
Bank fees & service charges	$15.00	$55.00	$47.00
Uniforms	$88.58	$267.93	$107.34
Total general business expenses	$103.58	$322.93	$154.34
Insurance	$175.00	$175.00	$175.00
Interest paid	$149.35	$151.18	$150.45
Legal & accounting services	$395.00	$454.00	$415.00
Meals	$279.59	$177.33	$138.44
Merchant fees	$1,485.31	$3,218.06	$2,685.39
Office expenses			
Office supplies	$152.84	$211.91	$137.08
Tech & software	$859.37	$725.13	$653.90
Total office expenses	$1,012.21	$937.04	$790.98
Payroll expenses			
Payroll processing fees	$226.00	$226.00	$226.00
Wages	$11,995.40	$16,805.28	$12,495.08
Total payroll expenses	$12,221.40	$17,031.28	$12,721.08
Rent	$6,000.00	$6,000.00	$6,000.00
Shrinkage	$39.00	$75.00	$89.00
Taxes paid			
Sales tax paid	$2,874.19	$3,472.94	$3,021.48
Payroll taxes—employer paid	$1,130.07	$1,597.16	$1,218.58
Total taxes paid	$4,004.26	$5,070.10	$4,240.06
Utilities	$389.62	$338.74	$307.55
Total expenses	**$27,229.32**	**$35,360.66**	**$29,037.29**
Net operating income	**$18,660.66**	**$47,278.27**	**$31,486.20**
Other income			
Credit card rewards	$38.12	$57.48	$42.90
Interest earned	$8.72	$14.46	$12.97
Total other income	$46.84	$71.94	$55.87
Net other income	**$46.84**	**$71.94**	**$55.87**
Net income	**$18,707.50**	**$47,350.21**	**$31,542.07**

Location Comparison

If your business has multiple locations, a location comparison P&L can be invaluable. This type of P&L evaluates the performance of each location, identifies strengths and weaknesses, and guides operation optimizations. The core components include the following:

- Revenue—compares the income generated by each location, highlighting which locations are performing well and which are underperforming

- Expenses—analyzes the costs incurred at each location, including rent, utilities, salaries, and other operational expenses, allowing for a comparison of cost efficiency

- Gross Profit—calculates the gross profit (revenue minus COGS) for each location, showing the profitability before accounting for operating expenses

- Net Profit—provides the net profit (gross profit minus operating expenses) for each location, offering a clear picture of the overall financial health of each branch

- Performance Metrics—includes various financial ratios and metrics, such as profit margins, return on investment (ROI), and break-even analysis for each location

Using a location comparison P&L, businesses can do the following:

- Identify high-performing locations and replicate successful strategies across other locations.

- Pinpoint underperforming locations and develop targeted improvement plans.

- Guide strategic adjustments regarding resource allocation, investments, and potential closures or expansions.

- Track the influence of local market conditions, competition, and other external factors on each location's financial performance.

A&J's Boutique
P&L Statement Cash Basis
Location Comparison
Oct 1, 2024 to Dec 31, 2024

	Location 1	Location 2	Overhead	Total
Income				
Sales revenue				
Basic apparel	$18,264.93	$27,071.28	$0.00	$45,336.21
Footwear	$10,974.22	$19,909.06	$0.00	$30,883.28
Children's clothing	$6,873.55	$12,093.78	$0.00	$18,967.33
Seasonal apparel and accessories	$11,839.52	$16,904.70	$0.00	$28,744.22
Home decor	$987.19	$13,335.59	$0.00	$14,322.78
Total sales revenue	$48,939.41	$89,314.41	$0.00	$138,253.82
Returns and allowances	-$281.85	-$902.80	$0.00	-$1,184.65
Total income	**$48,657.56**	**$88,411.61**	**$0.00**	**$137,069.17**
Cost of goods sold				
Products & inventory sold	$22,845.10	$31,375.45	$0.00	$54,220.55
Freight & shipping	$25.00	$62.00	$0.00	$87.00
Shopping bags & price tags	$39.23	$83.46	$0.00	$122.69
Total cost of goods sold	**$22,909.33**	**$31,520.91**	**$0.00**	**$54,430.24**
Gross profit	**$25,748.23**	**$56,890.70**	**$0.00**	**$82,638.93**
Expenses				
Advertising & marketing	$0.00	$0.00	$1,355.00	$1,355.00
Business licences & registration	$0.00	$0.00	$55.00	$55.00
General business expenses				$0.00
Bank fees & service charges	$0.00	$0.00	$55.00	$55.00
Uniforms	$119.01	$148.92	$0.00	$267.93
Total general business expenses	$119.01	$148.92	$55.00	$322.93
Insurance	$0.00	$0.00	$175.00	$175.00
Interest paid	$0.00	$0.00	$151.18	$151.18
Legal & accounting services	$0.00	$0.00	$454.00	$454.00
Meals	$73.45	$103.88	$0.00	$177.33
Merchant fees	$1,083.45	$2,134.61	$0.00	$3,218.06
Office expenses				
Office supplies	$72.40	$139.51	$0.00	$211.91
Tech & software	$0.00	$0.00	$725.13	$725.13
Total office expenses	$72.40	$139.51	$725.13	$937.04
Payroll expenses				
Payroll processing fees	$0.00	$0.00	$226.00	$226.00
Wages	$7,135.10	$9,670.18	$0.00	$16,805.28
Total payroll expenses	$7,135.10	$9,670.18	$226.00	$17,031.28
Rent	$3,000.00	$3,000.00	$0.00	$6,000.00
Shrinkage	$19.00	$56.00	$0.00	$75.00
Taxes paid				
Sales tax paid	$1,074.19	$2,398.75	$0.00	$3,472.94
Payroll taxes—employer paid	$630.07	$967.09	$0.00	$1,597.16
Total taxes paid	$1,704.26	$3,365.84	$0.00	$5,070.10
Utilities	$107.02	$231.72	$0.00	$338.74
Total expenses	**$13,313.69**	**$18,850.66**	**$3,196.31**	**$35,360.66**
Net operating income	**$12,434.54**	**$38,040.04**	**-$3,196.31**	**$47,278.27**
Other income				
Credit card rewards	$0.00	$0.00	$57.48	$57.48
Interest earned	$0.00	$0.00	$14.46	$14.46
Total other income	$0.00	$0.00	$71.94	$71.94
Net other income	**$0.00**	**$0.00**	**$71.94**	**$71.94**
Net income	**$12,434.54**	**$38,040.04**	**-$3,124.37**	**$47,350.21**

Percentage of Revenue

Percentages on a P&L show the proportion of each line item relative to total revenue, indicating how much each subaccount contributes to overall financial performance or what percentage of revenue is spent on a specific expense category.

This is calculated by dividing each line item by the total revenue and then multiplying by 100. These percentages analyze profitability, cost management, and operational efficiency by highlighting areas in need of attention or improvement.

Formulas:

Revenue Subaccount / Revenue x 100

COGS Subaccount / Revenue x 100

Expense Account / Revenue x 100

In the below example, each line item is divided by the total income amount of $245,798.66.

Joe's Woodworking
P&L Statement Cash Basis

Jan 1, 2024 to Dec 31, 2024
Percentage of Revenue

	1/1/24–12/31/24	% of Revenue
Income		
Revenue (direct sales)		
Bookcases	$38,750.77	15.77%
Coffee tables	$55,892.55	22.74%
Custom work	$125,178.10	50.93%
Total revenue (direct sales)	$219,821.42	89.43%
Wholesale revenue	$25,977.24	10.57%
Total income	**$245,798.66**	
Cost of goods sold		
Depreciation of equipment	$1,900.00	0.77%
Equipment maintenance	$2,890.07	1.18%
Labor	$40,000.00	16.27%
Supplies & materials	$64,722.68	26.33%
Total cost of goods sold	**$109,512.75**	**44.55%**
Gross profit	**$136,285.91**	
Expenses		
Advertising & marketing	$3,485.00	1.42%
Bank fees & service charges	$85.00	0.03%
Business licences & registration	$590.00	0.24%
General business expenses	$392.11	0.16%
Insurance	$6,500.00	2.64%
Interest paid	$1,284.93	0.52%
Legal & accounting services		
Accounting fees	$1,750.00	0.71%
Legal fees	$890.00	0.36%
Total legal & accounting services	$2,640.00	1.07%
Office expenses		
Office supplies	$2,306.22	0.94%
Small tools and equipment	$1,578.45	0.64%
Tech & software	$576.81	0.23%
Total office expenses	$4,461.48	1.82%
Payroll processing fee	$540.00	0.22%
Taxes paid		
Sales tax paid	$12,287.42	5.00%
Payroll taxes—employer paid	$3,825.85	1.56%
Property tax	$1,875.92	0.76%
Total taxes paid	$17,989.19	7.32%
Utilities	$3,781.60	1.54%
Total expenses	**$41,749.31**	**16.99%**
Net operating income	**$94,536.60**	
Other income		
Credit card rewards	$150.00	
Interest earned	$48.29	
Total other income	$198.29	
Net other income	**$198.29**	
Net income	**$94,734.89**	

Profit Margin

Your P&L provides the data needed to calculate your profit margin. There are three profit margins to consider: gross profit, operating, and net profit margins. These financial ratios are expressed as percentages and indicate whether you are meeting, exceeding, or falling short of your revenue goals.

Gross Profit Margin

Gross profit margin calculates the percentage of revenue remaining *after* covering COGS but *before* accounting for operating expenses. A higher margin suggests efficient production and strong pricing power, helping you assess production costs and refine pricing strategies.

Formula:

(Revenue – COGS) / Revenue x 100

Operating Profit Margin

Operating profit margin represents the percentage of revenue left after covering COGS and operating expenses (e.g., salaries and rent), excluding interest and taxes. This metric highlights the efficiency of your core operations, with a higher operating margin signaling better control of operational costs. Reviewing this margin helps assess how well you manage operating expenses.

Formula:

Operating Income / Revenue x 100

Net Profit Margin

Net profit margin shows the percentage of revenue left as profit after all expenses, including COGS, operating costs, interest, and taxes. This ratio provides insight into overall profitability and how efficiently revenue is converted into profit. A higher margin reflects strong cost control, while a lower margin may highlight areas needing improvement for long-term sustainability.

Formula:

Net Profit / Revenue x 100

Examining all three profit margins provides valuable insights into different aspects of financial health, pointing to where costs are incurred and how effectively revenue is converted into profit at different stages of the P&L.

Using Joe's Woodworking as an example, here are the three types of margins.

Gross Profit Margin

(245,798.66 - 109,512.75) / 245,798.66 x 100 = 55.45%

Operating Profit Margin

$94,536.60 / 245,798.66 x 100 = 38.46%

Net Profit Margin

$94,734.89 / 245,798.66 x 100 = 38.54%

(One additional type of comparative analysis to conduct with your P&L is a budget versus actual report. This will be covered in Chapter 15, which is all about budgets.)

Chapter Highlights

- Profit and Loss Statement (P&L)—a P&L is a summary of your company's earnings and expenses over a specific period, displaying net profit or loss.

- Check for Accuracy—verify that revenue, COGS, and expenses are correctly categorized, loan payments and owner distributions are excluded, and anomalies are investigated.

- Analyze the P&L—assess revenue streams, cost efficiencies, unnecessary expenses, and net income fluctuations for profitability improvement.

- Job Costing—track individual project costs and profits to refine pricing, optimize costs, and gauge the profitability of projects.

- Comparative Analysis—compare financials by YTD, time frame, location, or percentage of revenue to identify trends and growth opportunities.

- Profit Margin—use profit margins (gross, operating, and net profit) to evaluate cost efficiency, pricing strategies, operational performance, and overall financial health.

Chapter Eleven

Balance Sheet

The balance sheet is one of the most commonly overlooked and misunderstood financial reports by small business owners. Throughout my experience working with small businesses, I've repeatedly witnessed how a lack of understanding of the balance sheet can result in poor financial choices and, in some cases, business failure. Small business owners tend to focus only on the P&L or cash flow statements. This oversight can lead to a distorted view of your business's financial state.

Your balance sheet is a fundamental financial statement providing a snapshot of your small business's financial position at a specific point in time. Based on the accounting equation, this statement shows the relationship between three components: assets, liabilities, and equity. It clearly outlines what your company owns (assets), what it owes (liabilities), and the residual claim of the owners (equity). (Refer to Chapter 7 for more details about the accounting equation and the specific components included.)

Assets: what you own

Liabilities: what you owe

Equity: the difference between the two

Take the time to familiarize yourself with the items on a balance sheet, learn how to interpret the information, and use it to guide your business strategy. Whether seeking financing, evaluating investment opportunities, or monitoring fiscal well-being, the balance sheet is a crucial resource for stability, growth, and long-term success.

Does it have to balance?

First, let's discuss the reason it's called a balance sheet—it must balance!

Assets = Liabilities + Equity

If all bookkeeping entries are done correctly, your balance sheet will be balanced based on the accounting equation (see Chapter 7). To recap, this equation expresses the fundamental principle of double-entry accounting, which requires every transaction to have two sides: a debit and a credit.

Let's look at examples from each of the small businesses we're following, which illustrate how financial transactions affect the balance sheet.

Example 1

Joe's Woodworking purchased a new saw for $5,000 with cash from the checking account. In this example, two asset accounts are impacted—one is debited and the other is credited. Thus, both sides of the transaction are recorded within the asset category.

- Assets decrease with a credit: The checking account funds used to purchase the equipment are now reduced on the balance sheet.

- Assets increase with a debit: The equipment purchased is now an asset on the balance sheet

Account Name	Debit	Credit
Checking Account		$5,000
Equipment	$5,000	

Example 2

The owners of A&J's Boutique take an owners' distribution from the business each month. Owner A and Owner J each take $3,000. This transaction shows how the impact on the asset account is balanced by the adjustment to the equity side of the equation.

- Assets decrease with a credit: The cash amount on the balance sheet is reduced by the $6,000 withdrawn.

- Equity decreases with a debit: Each owner's equity is reduced by $3,000.

Account Name	Debit	Credit
Checking Account		$6,000
Owner Distribution: A	$3,000	
Owner Distribution: J	$3,000	

Example 3

The Marketing Group has obtained a $10,000 bank loan to assist with startup costs. This transaction is balanced by adjusting both liabilities and assets.

- Assets increase with a debit: The cash received from the loan is now an asset on the balance sheet.

- Liabilities increase with a credit: The principal balance of the loan is now a liability on the balance sheet.

Account Name	Debit	Credit
Checking Account	$10,000	
Loan		$10,000

In these examples, the fundamental accounting equation of Assets = Liabilities + Equity is maintained. The balance sheet continues to balance after the transactions are recorded, demonstrating its importance in accurately reflecting a company's financial position. Maintaining this balance provides reliability and transparency and supports effective oversight. It also assures stakeholders that the business's resources and financing are correctly accounted for, ensuring the integrity of the financial statements.

Next, we'll discuss the specific details of how the balance sheet is created.

This report is ongoing—always accumulating. The beginning date is when the company was established, after which the balance sheet is presented "as of" a specific date. The assets are listed first, followed by the liabilities, and then the equity. This allows you to see at a glance the balance, or value, of each item on the balance sheet.

Here is a list of the individual components typically found on a small business balance sheet in the order they should be listed. This is not a fully exhaustive list, but it is what you will most likely see on your balance sheet. (Refer to Chapter 7 for a detailed explanation of each component.)

Assets

- Current Assets

    ◦ Cash and Cash Equivalents/Bank Accounts

    ◦ Accounts Receivable

    ◦ Inventory

- Noncurrent Assets

    ◦ Property, Plant, and Equipment (PP&E)

    ◦ Intangible Assets

    ◦ Investments

Liabilities

- Current Liabilities

    ◦ Accounts Payable

    ◦ Short-term Loans/Credit Cards

    ◦ Accrued Expenses

- ○ Unearned Revenue
- • Noncurrent Liabilities

  - ○ Long-term Loans

  - ○ Deferred Tax Liabilities

  - ○ Leases

  - ○ Loans from Owner

Equity

- • Owner/Shareholder Contributions/Investments

- • Owner/Shareholder Distributions

- • Retained Earnings

- • Net Income

Because the last two equity items were not fully covered in the earlier chapter, let's spend a moment looking into their specifics.

Retained Earnings

The retained earnings line represents the accumulated net income from previous years after distributions to owners or shareholders. These profits are reinvested (retained) in the company rather than paid out as distributions (or dividends). This line shows the cumulative net profits that have been saved within the business since its inception, indicating how much of the company's profits have been reinvested over time.

Net Income

The net income is data taken from your P&L for the current year. This figure is the total amount after subtracting all your expenses from your revenue. If you have more money left over after expenses, you've made a profit, and this number will be positive. If you've spent more money than you made, you have experienced a loss, and this number will be negative. At the end of your fiscal year, this amount will be reflected in the retained earnings line.

In the example below, you can see how the owner equity accounts and net income are closed out at the end of the year to the retained earnings line, but the total equity value remains the same.

	12/31/24	1/1/25
Equity		
Owner contribution	$25,000.00	$0.00
Owner distribution	-$72,000.00	$0.00
Retained earnings	$19,153.18	$66,888.07
Net income	$94,734.89	$0.00
Total equity	**$66,888.07**	**$66,888.07**

Retained earnings and net income are two types of equity small businesses may have, depending on the ownership interests and capital structure of the company. The specific types of equity present in a small business will depend on the business's legal structure, ownership arrangements, and financing history.

As mentioned in the earlier chapter, if you have an S or C corp, the terms used in the equity portion of your balance sheet will be *shareholder(s)* instead of *owner(s)*. Also, a corporation may have shareholder dividends that are paid out.

Opening Balance Equity

This is not a formal accounting term, but I'll share about it because some accounting software uses it as a temporary holding account and will auto-generate transactions with it.

Opening balance equity is a placeholder for the difference between credit and debit balances, ensuring that the accounting equation is balanced. It is most often seen when you first start using accounting software or when particular assets or liabilities are added to the books, but the entry isn't balanced correctly.

Over time, the opening balance equity account should be cleared out and allocated to the appropriate accounts. This is another situation when professional help is beneficial.

Key Items to Verify Accuracy

When reviewing your balance sheet, inspect the following elements to be certain your information is reliable:

Cash and Cash Equivalents

- Confirm that the reported cash (and cash equivalents) figures match the bank statements.

- Check for discrepancies—any differences may indicate cash management or accounting issues.

Accounts Receivable

- Review the aging of receivables to identify potential collection issues. (See Chapter 13 for how to run an aging report.)

- Inspect for correctness and ensure that receivables are not overstated.

Inventory

- Compare physical inventory counts to the balance sheet, investigate discrepancies, and be certain inventory is valued using your chosen accounting method (e.g., FIFO, LIFO).

- Verify that damaged and/or missing inventory is reported as shrinkage and moved to the P&L.

- Check that the appropriate amount has been moved from the inventory account to COGS for the financial reporting period. Reconcile with the numbers reported on your P&L.

Liabilities

- Review accounts payable to confirm that all obligations are accurately recorded and classified.

- Ensure that loan/debt payments are recorded accurately, with interest expenses on the P&L and only principal payments on the balance sheet.

Equity

- Be certain that all contributions and withdrawals by owners/shareholders are accurately recorded and that revenue and expenses haven't been incorrectly categorized as owner/shareholder investments and distributions.

- Assess the retained earnings line to verify that it represents the accumulation of net income (or losses) and your company's profitability and reinvestment choices.

Finally, be certain that the balance sheet is consistent with your P&L and cash flow statements. By carefully examining these elements, you can have confidence in your balance sheet to provide reliable data.

Analysis Strategies

Having verified the balance sheet's accuracy, the next step is to analyze it. As stated, the balance sheet is frequently misunderstood and overlooked. I suggest giving priority to its analysis.

When reviewing your company's balance sheet, consider the following questions:

Liquidity

- Do I have enough current assets (e.g., cash, receivables) to cover my current liabilities?

- How quickly can my assets be converted into cash if needed?

Debt Management

- What is the ratio of my company's debt to equity? Is my company relying too much on external financing?

- Are there upcoming debt obligations that might strain my cash flow?

Asset Management

- Are my assets appropriately valued, and do they represent their true market value?

- Is my inventory turning over efficiently, or is too much money tied up in slow-moving stock?

- Are there nonproductive assets that could be liquidated or better utilized?

Equity and Owner Investment

- How does my company's current retained earnings compare to previous periods? Is the business growing its equity?

- Is there enough equity to support future growth or expansion plans?

- Has there been a significant change in owner's equity? What is driving this change—profits, additional investments, or the need for personal withdrawals?

Incorporating your balance sheet into your financial review process fosters growth and profitability. Here's why:

- Financial Monitoring—your balance sheet assesses financial health by comparing assets and liabilities, evaluating liquidity, and ensuring the ability to meet short-term obligations. This aids in addressing potential challenges proactively.

- Access to Financing—lenders and investors rely heavily on balance sheet data to gauge a small business's stability and risk profile. Maintaining a reliable and up-to-date balance sheet can significantly enhance your chances of securing favorable financing terms.

- Compliance and Reporting—depending on your tax classification and income level, you may be required to include a balance sheet with your financial statements for tax reporting and regulatory compliance. Regardless of this requirement, a good tax professional will want to see your balance sheet to verify accurate bookkeeping year over year.

- Business Valuation—a current balance sheet is integral when valuing a business for purposes like mergers, sales, and franchise opportunities. It provides financial data used to appraise the business's true worth and fair market value.

Joe's Woodworking
Balance Sheet
As of Dec 31, 2024

ASSETS

Current assets	
Bank accounts	
Checking	$3,107.83
Savings	$8,240.15
Total bank accounts	$11,347.98
Raw materials	$2,409.33
Inventory	$3,750.00
Total current assets	**$17,507.31**
Fixed assets	
Tools & equipment	$10,100.00
Workshop building	$200,000.00
Total fixed assets	**$210,100.00**
TOTAL ASSETS	**$227,607.31**
LIABILITIES AND EQUITY	
Liabilities	
Current liabilities	
Credit card	$1,299.82
Sales tax payable	$1,200.00
Total current liabilities	**$2,499.82**
Long-term liabilities	
Bank loan	$8,324.87
Workshop mortgage	$149,894.55
Total long-term liabilities	**$158,219.42**
Total liabilities	**$160,719.24**
Equity	
Owner contribution	$25,000.00
Owner distribution	-$72,000.00
Retained earnings	$19,153.18
Net income	$94,734.89
Total equity	**$66,888.07**
TOTAL LIABILITIES AND EQUITY	**$227,607.31**

A&J's Boutique

Balance Sheet

As of 12/31/2024

ASSETS

Current assets	
Checking	$13,922.11
Inventory	$16,133.73
Total current assets	**$30,055.84**
Noncurrent assets	
Shelving & furniture	$8,932.94
Total noncurrent assets	**$8,932.94**
TOTAL ASSETS	**$38,988.78**
LIABILITIES AND EQUITY	
Liabilities	
Current liabilities	
Credit card	$1,245.09
Bank loan	$10,000.00
Sales tax payable	$295.84
Total current liabilities	**$11,540.93**
Equity	
Owner contribution: A	$10,000.00
Owner contribution: J	$10,000.00
Owner distribution: A	-$24,750.00
Owner distribution: J	-$24,750.00
Retained earnings	$9,597.64
Net income	$47,350.21
Total equity	**$27,447.85**
TOTAL LIABILITIES AND EQUITY	**$38,988.78**

The Marketing Group
Balance Sheet
As of 12/31/2024

ASSETS	
Current assets	
Bank accounts	
Checking	$7,813.36
Savings	$23,544.55
Total bank accounts	$31,357.91
Accounts receivable	$54,750.00
Total current assets	**$86,107.91**
TOTAL ASSETS	**$86,107.91**
LIABILITIES AND EQUITY	
Liabilities	
Current liabilities	
Credit card *1234	$1,094.56
Credit card *2345	$821.46
Credit card *3456	$306.77
Total credit cards	$2,222.79
Unearned revenue	$2,000.00
Total current liabilities	**$4,222.79**
Total liabilities	**$4,222.79**
Equity	
Shareholder contribution	$0.00
Shareholder distribution	-$28,750.00
Retained earnings	$98,106.37
Net income	$12,528.75
Total equity	**$81,885.12**
TOTAL LIABILITIES AND EQUITY	**$86,107.91**

Chapter Highlights:

- Balance Sheet—based on the accounting equation (Assets = Liabilities + Equity) the balance sheet provides a snapshot of your business's financial position.

- Retained Earnings—when cumulative net profits are reinvested in the company (instead of distributed to owners/shareholders), they are called retained earnings. This figure reflects the amount of profit retained and reinvested since the business's establishment.

- Check for Accuracy—verify that cash, receivables, inventory, liabilities, and equity are correctly recorded.

- Financial Stability—evaluate your company's liquidity, debt management, and equity growth.

Chapter Twelve

Cash Flow Statement

Having discussed the elements of the P&L and the balance sheet, we can now turn our attention to the cash flow statement, which combines data from both. Similar to the P&L, this statement covers a specific period (month, year, etc.), often labeled "for the month ended..." or "as of..." True to its name, the cash flow statement illustrates the movement of cash into and out of your business.

The cash flow statement allows you to quickly see what areas are generating and using the most cash in your company (most often the operating activities). The numbers in this report can assist with forecasting revenue and expenses, identifying seasonal patterns, and creating budgets. Your cash flow statement is a central component of financial analysis, providing insights into a company's liquidity, solvency, and cash generation.

It is divided into three segments:

1. Operating Activities—cash flows associated with core business operations (the day-to-day transactions that allow the company to cover its operational costs and

maintain its main business activities), the selling of products and services, and the associated expenses

2. Investing Activities—cash flows related to the purchasing, selling, and investment in long-term assets, such as equipment, property, and vehicles

3. Financing Activities—cash flows related to debt, equity, and dividend transactions, including incoming money from loans and owner investments, as well as outflows for loan payments and owner distributions

At the end of each segment, the net cash flow is calculated to determine the overall movement of cash (and cash equivalents) for the period. Reporting all the cash added or used by the company, the cash flow statement displays the cash balance at the start and end of the period alongside the change in cash.

For the two previous reports (P&L and balance sheet), we walked through the steps to verify accuracy. If you have done this for both of those reports, then there are no additional items to check on the cash flow statement because the data is pulled from the same sources.

Analysis Strategies

Reviewing your cash flow statement will allow you to stay attuned to your financial dynamics, make timely adjustments, and optimize long-term sustainability and profitability. When analyzing your cash flow statement, consider asking yourself the following questions:

- Is the company consistently bringing in more cash than it is spending?

- If the cash flow is negative, what are the main reasons?

- Which areas of the business are generating the most cash? Are these sources sustainable and reliable?

- Is my business generating enough cash from its core operations?

- Where is most of the cash going? Are these expenditures necessary, or is it possible to reduce these expenses/withdrawals?

- Can the business comfortably handle unexpected expenses or slow periods?

- How does my cash flow compare to previous periods?

- How long can the business sustain operations at this pace?

Here are the top reasons why you should review your cash flow statement:

- Monitor Liquidity and Obligations—be certain you have enough cash on hand to cover operational expenses, pay bills, and meet other short-term obligations. This helps prevent cash shortages.

- Identify Cash Flow Trends—discover irregularities in cash flow patterns, such as seasonal fluctuations and unexpected drops. Early identification of these issues allows you to take corrective actions and adjust your cash management strategy, including investment planning, debt repayment, and resource allocation.

- Informed Financial Planning—evaluate your ability to generate cash, pay debt, and fund growth. This supports more effective financial planning and budgeting, enabling you to allocate resources wisely and plan for future investments and/or expansions.

Joe's Woodworking

Cash Flow Statement

Jan 1, 2024 to Dec 31, 2024

Cash at beginning of period	$4,986.03
OPERATING ACTIVITIES	
Net income	$94,734.89
Depreciation	$1,900.00
Credit card	$1,391.29
Sales tax	$349.95
Raw materials & inventory	-$14,170.60
Net cash provided by operating activities	**$84,205.53**
INVESTING ACTIVITIES	
Tools & equipment	-$8,000.00
Net cash provided by investing activities	**-$8,000.00**
FINANCING ACTIVITIES	
Bank loan	$7,324.87
Workshop mortgage	-$30,168.45
Owner contribution	$25,000.00
Owner distribution	-$72,000.00
Net cash provided by financing activities	**-$69,843.58**
Net cash increase for period	**$6,361.95**
Cash at end of period	**$11,347.98**

A&J's Boutique

Cash Flow Statement

Oct 1, 2024 to Dec 31, 2024

Cash at beginning of period	$4,409.20
OPERATING ACTIVITIES	
Net income	$47,350.21
Credit card	$2,640.91
Sales tax	$895.16
Inventory	-$11,873.37
Net cash provided by operating activities	**$39,012.91**
INVESTING ACTIVITIES	
N/A	$0.00
Net cash provided by investing activities	**$0.00**
FINANCING ACTIVITIES	
Bank loan	$10,000.00
Owner contribution: A	$10,000.00
Owner contribution: J	$10,000.00
Owner distribution: A	-$24,750.00
Owner distribution: J	-$24,750.00
Net cash provided by financing activities	**-$29,500.00**
Net cash increase for period	**$9,512.91**
Cash at end of period	**$13,922.11**

The Marketing Group
Cash Flow Statement
Dec 1, 2024 to Dec 31, 2024

Cash at beginning of period	$34,295.95
OPERATING ACTIVITIES	
Net income	$12,528.75
Accounts receivable (A/R)	$7,575.00
Credit cards	$5,708.21
Net cash provided by operating activities	**$25,811.96**
INVESTING ACTIVITIES	
N/A	$0.00
Net cash provided by investing activities	**$0.00**
FINANCING ACTIVITIES	
Shareholder contribution	$0.00
Shareholder distribution	-$28,750.00
Net cash provided by financing activities	**-$28,750.00**
Net cash increase for period	**-$2,938.04**
Cash at end of period	**$31,357.91**

How are the three financial statements linked?

The three main financial statements—balance sheet, P&L, and cash flow statements—are intricately linked, offering complementary perspectives on a company's financial performance and position, with each statement influencing and displaying data from the others.

P&L and Balance Sheet

The net income figure from your P&L is carried over to the balance sheet and moved into retained earnings after the end of the year, affecting your equity.

Balance Sheet and Cash Flow Statement

Changes in balance sheet accounts, including accounts receivable, accounts payable, and inventory, are reflected in your cash flow statement to indicate the movement of cash. For example, securing a new loan from the bank will increase your liabilities on the balance sheet while also showing the influx of cash in the financing portion of the cash flow statement.

Cash Flow Statement and P&L

The cash flow statement starts with the net income figure from the P&L.

Make it a priority to regularly assess these reports, ideally every month. Consistently reviewing your financials enables you to spot trends, implement strategic adjustments, and address potential issues early on. A clear understanding of your business's financial health will support wise business choices and continue the pursuit of your personal and business goals.

Chapter Highlights

- Cash Flow Statement—tracks the inflow and outflow of cash over a specific period

- Three Segments of a Cash Flow Statement—operating, investing, and financing activities

- Analyze Cash Flow—to identify which areas generate or consume the most cash

- Three Main Financial Statements—balance sheet, P&L, and cash flow statement are interconnected and display shared data

Chapter Thirteen

Supplementary Reports

In addition to the three primary statements, your bookkeeping can also produce supplementary reports, which provide thorough analyses of specific financial aspects. These reports offer deeper insights into the various elements of the main financial statements.

The following supplementary reports are strongly suggested for regular monitoring of your business finances. Your selection of reports will vary based on the nature of your business, its structure, the products you offer, if you have employees, and whether you invoice your clients.

Accounts Receivable Aging Report

The accounts receivable aging report provides a detailed snapshot of your company's unpaid invoices, categorizing them by how long they've been outstanding—typically thirty, sixty, ninety days, and beyond. This report includes a "current" column indicating the invoice is not due yet. For example, when the payment terms are net 30, the invoice will show in the current column for thirty days. After that, it will move to the next column labeled "1 – 30."

This report serves multiple purposes:

- Cash Flow Management—highlights overdue invoices, allowing you to identify late-paying customers and prioritize collection efforts, thereby improving cash flow

- Credit Risk Assessment—offers awareness of customer payment behavior, helping you decide whether to extend credit or require upfront payments in the future

- Accounting and Reporting—required for accurate financial reporting and ensuring compliance with accounting standards

Mismanagement of accounts receivable can cause ongoing cash flow challenges for small businesses, as delayed payments restrict your ability to cover operating expenses. If overdue collections are a recurring issue, consider reviewing the accounts receivable aging report weekly to resolve it. The older a debt becomes, the less likely it is to be collected, making prompt action critical.

The Marketing Group
Accounts Receivable Aging Report
As of Dec 31, 2024

	Current	1 - 30	31 - 60	61 - 90	91 and over	Total
Client 1	$5,750.00					$5,750.00
Client 2	$11,000.00					$11,000.00
Client 3			$13,220.00			$13,220.00
Client 4				$12,880.00		$12,880.00
Client 5		$2,500.00				$2,500.00
Client 6		$7,500.00				$7,500.00
Client 7	$1,900.00					$1,900.00
TOTAL	$18,650.00	$10,000.00	$13,220.00	$12,880.00	$0.00	$54,750.00

Accounts Payable Aging Report

An accounts payable report provides a comprehensive view of your company's outstanding bills, detailing how much you owe, to whom, and how long the payments have been due. This report assists with controlling short-term financial obligations and tracking cash flow. It guides you to prioritize payments, ensuring that you pay the right vendors at the right time. Similar to the accounts receivable aging report, the accounts payable report is typically broken down into thirty-day increments.

Reviewing this report ensures that your business pays its bills on time, avoids late fees, and maintains strong relationships with suppliers. Additionally, the accounts payable report can uncover discrepancies or errors in your accounts, allowing for timely corrections, improving financial accuracy, and prioritizing financial obligations.

A&J's Boutique
Accounts Payable Aging Report
As of Dec 31, 2024

	Current	1 - 30	31 - 60	61 - 90	91 and over	Total
Vendor 1	$109.50					$109.50
Vendor 2		$60.00				$60.00
Vendor 3			$89.99			$89.99
Vendor 4	$822.44					$822.44
Vendor 5	$550.00					$550.00
TOTAL	$1,481.94	$60.00	$89.99	$0.00	$0.00	$1,631.93

Sales Report

The sales report includes data on sales revenue, unit sales, and relevant trends observed over a specific period, in most cases a month, a quarter, or a year. This information can be further broken down by product, customer, or sales representative, enabling granular analysis of sales performance. By analyzing the sales report data, you can identify strengths and weaknesses; guide strategic adjustments to offerings, pricing, and marketing; and allocate resources more effectively.

Joe's Woodworking
Sales Report
July 1, 2024 to Dec 31, 2024

Product #	Product Description	Category	Qty	Price	Sales
BKW301	3 Shelf 32h 32w Walnut	Bookcases	4	$479.99	$1,919.96
BKM301	3 Shelf 32h 32w Maple	Bookcases	1	$479.99	$479.99
BKC301	3 Shelf 32h 32w Cherry	Bookcases	2	$479.99	$959.98
BKW501	5 Shelf 52h 24w Walnut	Bookcases	3	$899.99	$2,699.97
BKM501	5 Shelf 52h 24w Maple	Bookcases	4	$899.99	$3,599.96
BKC501	5 Shelf 52h 24w Cherry	Bookcases	1	$899.99	$899.99
BKW502	5 Shelf 52h 12w Walnut	Bookcases	5	$675.99	$3,379.95
BKM502	5 Shelf 52h 12w Maple	Bookcases	2	$675.99	$1,351.98
BKC502	5 Shelf 52h 12w Cherry	Bookcases	4	$675.99	$2,703.96
BKW601	6 Shelf 70h 24w Walnut	Bookcases	1	$999.99	$999.99
BKM601	6 Shelf 70h 24w Maple	Bookcases	2	$999.99	$1,999.98
BKC601	6 Shelf 70h 24w Cherry	Bookcases	3	$999.99	$2,999.97
CTOW01	30in Oval Walnut	Coffee tables	5	$399.99	$1,999.95
CTOM01	30in Oval Maple	Coffee tables	7	$399.99	$2,799.93
CTOC01	30in Oval Cherry	Coffee tables	3	$399.99	$1,199.97
CTOW02	50in Oval Walnut	Coffee tables	8	$599.99	$4,799.92
CTOM02	50in Oval Maple	Coffee tables	6	$599.99	$3,599.94
CTOC02	50in Oval Cherry	Coffee tables	4	$599.99	$2,399.96
CTRW01	40in Rectangle Walnut	Coffee tables	5	$489.99	$2,449.95
CTRM01	40in Rectangle Maple	Coffee tables	2	$489.99	$979.98
CTRC01	40in Rectangle Cherry	Coffee tables	7	$489.99	$3,429.93
Total					**$47,655.21**

Inventory Report

Accurate inventory tracking is necessary for efficient stock control and purchasing processes. Keeping tabs on current inventory levels, costs, and turnover rates helps you maintain optimal stock levels. This report will distinguish between overstocked and understocked items as well as fast- and slow-moving products. Utilizing this data empowers you to make strategic choices based on facts, ensuring product availability, reducing surplus inventory, and improving operational efficiency.

A&J's Boutique
Inventory Report
July 1, 2024 to Sep 30, 2024

Product ID	Product Category	Product Name	Beginning Qty	Qty Sold	Balance	Cost	Price
YRJ01	Children's clothing	Youth Rain Jacket XS	9	2	7	$18.00	$32.99
YRJ02	Children's clothing	Youth Rain Jacket S	19	9	10	$18.00	$32.99
YRJ03	Children's clothing	Youth Rain Jacket M	18	4	14	$18.00	$32.99
YRJ04	Children's clothing	Youth Rain Jacket L	22	8	14	$18.00	$32.99
YRJ05	Children's clothing	Youth Rain Jacket XL	11	9	2	$18.00	$32.99
4JT01	Seasonal apparel and accessories	4th of July Tee XS	14	5	9	$12.00	$27.99
4JT02	Seasonal apparel and accessories	4th of July Tee S	10	3	7	$12.00	$27.99
4JT03	Seasonal apparel and accessories	4th of July Tee M	8	8	0	$12.00	$27.99
4JT04	Seasonal apparel and accessories	4th of July Tee L	9	9	0	$12.00	$27.99
4JT05	Seasonal apparel and accessories	4th of July Tee XL	13	4	9	$12.00	$27.99

Payroll Report

If you have employees, your payroll report provides a comprehensive breakdown of compensation, including hours worked, wages earned, taxes withheld, and other deductions. It plays a vital role in ensuring payroll accuracy and compliance. By reviewing this report, you can verify employee payments, ensure proper tax calculations, and streamline payroll processes. Proper tracking of this data helps you uphold labor law compliance and offers you a clear overview of employee compensation.

The Marketing Group
Payroll Report
Pay Period 7/1/24-7/14/24

	Gross Pay	Taxes Witheld	Net Pay	Employer Paid Taxes	Cash Required
Employee 1	$2,083.33	$312.50	$1,770.83	$145.83	$2,229.16
Employee 2	$3,333.33	$500.00	$2,833.33	$233.33	$3,566.66
Employee 3	$3,333.33	$666.67	$2,666.66	$233.33	$3,566.66
Employee 4	$2,083.33	$312.50	$1,770.83	$145.83	$2,229.16
Employee 5	$2,500.00	$375.00	$2,125.00	$175.00	$2,675.00
Employee 6	$3,750.00	$750.00	$3,000.00	$262.50	$4,012.50
	$17,083.32	$2,916.66	$14,166.66	$1,195.83	$18,279.15

Using accounting software enables you to generate virtually unlimited report variations tailored to specific needs. For example, you can create a report detailing all transactions with a particular vendor or view deposits over $5,000, grouped by customer. With up-to-date bookkeeping, all the data to support decision-making is readily available—as long as you know where to locate it. If you want to explore a particular aspect of your business, generate a report that provides the insights you're looking for.

The value of bookkeeping lies in generating reliable financial reports that can identify trends and inform discussions. Develop a clear, consistent, and repeatable process. The more frequently you do this, the more confident and comfortable you'll become in evaluating your business's numbers.

Chapter Highlights

- Additional Reports—offer detailed data derived from the three main financial statements, enhancing the oversight of specific financial components (examples follow)

- Accounts Receivable Aging Report—tracks overdue invoices, highlights potential cash flow issues, and aids in credit risk assessment

- Accounts Payable Report—displays outstanding bills, supports management of short-term obligations, and prioritizes vendor payments

- Sales Report—provides specifics of revenue, unit sales, and performance trends

- Inventory Report—monitors stock levels and turnover rates, optimizing purchasing decisions

- Payroll Report—details employee compensation and deductions, ensuring accurate payroll processing

Chapter Fourteen

Pricing Strategy

Determining an effective pricing strategy is one of the most challenging yet critical decisions for a small business, as it directly affects both profitability and market competitiveness. Building enough profit into your pricing is required for the long-term sustainability and growth of your business. Without accounting for all necessary items—operational costs, owner distributions (or wages, depending on entity type), taxes, employee benefits, and retirement savings—you risk running at a loss.

Profit allows your business to do the following:

- Cover unexpected expenses

- Invest in growth opportunities

- Support employee wages and benefits

- Provide for yourself as a business owner

- Ensure the long-term stability of the business

When setting prices, you must consider not only the cost of goods or services but also the broader financial picture. Insufficient profit margins may leave you unable to cover essential costs, hindering both your personal well-being and the future of your business. (Refer to Chapter 10 for a deeper dive into profit margins.) Prioritizing profitability from the outset is key to sustaining operations and thriving in the long term.

Follow these steps when crafting your pricing strategy:

Research the Market

The first step is to conduct thorough research on your competitors. Start by analyzing the prices of similar products or services within your industry. This includes not only direct competitors but also their pricing models and the factors influencing their rates.

By examining competitor pricing, you gain awareness of customer preferences and their willingness to pay for specific features or benefits. Some customers may prioritize premium offerings with enhanced services, while others may favor more affordable options with fewer features. For example, you might discover that customers are willing to pay more for eco-friendly products and exceptional customer service, indicating a trend toward valuing sustainability and support. Alternatively, if competitors are attracting price-sensitive consumers with basic offerings, affordability may be a driver in that market.

Understanding market demand helps establish profitable pricing. This research indicates how much consumers are willing to pay, as influenced by preferences, economic conditions, and spending patterns. High demand allows for higher prices, while low demand and stiff competition may require discounts or bundles. By staying adaptable to market shifts and monitoring competitors' pricing, you can set prices that attract customers while maintaining healthy profit margins. Aligning your pricing with both market conditions and customer expectations positions your business for long-term success.

Understand Your Costs

To set your prices effectively, identify the fixed and variable costs for your company.

Fixed or overhead costs are ongoing expenses necessary for the operation of your business but not directly tied to specific products or services. These costs include rent, utilities, insurance, and salaries for staff not directly involved in production. Even though these costs do not generate revenue on their own, they are essential in maintaining the infrastructure of your business. Failing to account for these expenses can lead you to underprice your products or services, ultimately jeopardizing your profitability.

On the other hand, variable costs are those that fluctuate based on the production volume of goods or services. This includes materials needed for production and labor costs associated with creating those goods or delivering those services. Accurately calculating these variable costs ensures that your pricing covers all expenses while also allowing you to achieve your desired profit margin.

By having a grasp on both fixed and variable costs, you can set prices that not only cover all operational expenses but also support sustainable business growth. (Refer to Chapter 6 for a more detailed explanation of costs/expenses.)

Consider the Value to Customers

Ask yourself what value your products or services provide to customers. Then, evaluate their unique benefits and how they set you apart from competitors. Values might include superior quality, exceptional customer service, innovative features, and a strong brand reputation. Being aware of these differentiators allows you to articulate the added value customers receive when choosing your offerings.

Once you have identified these benefits, price your products or services accordingly. Reflecting this added value in your pricing not only justifies higher prices but also builds customer loyalty and trust. Customers are often willing to pay a premium for products they perceive as offering greater value compared to alternatives in the market. By aligning your pricing with the distinct advantages of your offerings, you create a compelling proposition that resonates with consumers and enhances their overall experience with your brand.

Choose a Pricing Model

The pricing model you choose directly influences profitability and market positioning. Here are several common pricing strategies to consider:

- Cost-Plus Pricing—this straightforward approach involves adding a markup to your costs to build in profitability. By calculating the total cost of production and then determining a suitable profit margin, you can set prices to cover expenses while generating income.

- Value-Based Pricing—unlike cost-plus pricing, this model focuses on the customer's perceived value of a product or service rather than just its price. By recognizing what customers are willing to pay, you can set prices that represent this perception of value, potentially leading to higher profits.

- Competitive Pricing—in this strategy, you align your prices with those of competitors in the market. This approach is particularly useful in highly competitive industries in which price sensitivity is a factor. By monitoring competitors' pricing strategies, you can position your company effectively without losing market share.

- Penetration Pricing—this tactic involves starting with lower prices to attract customers and gain market entry quickly. Once a customer base is established and brand loyalty develops, you can gradually increase prices over time without losing your regular shoppers.

- Premium Pricing—setting higher prices indicates a product's high quality or exclusivity in premium pricing models. This strategy targets consumers who associate higher costs with superior products or services and are willing to pay more for perceived luxury or uniqueness.

Each of these pricing models has its advantages and considerations; selecting the right one depends on your business goals, target audience, and overall market conditions.

Monitor and Adjust

Once you've established your pricing, remember that it is not a one-time decision. Don't just set it and forget it; you must continuously monitor the effectiveness of your pricing strategy. The market is dynamic, and various factors influence how your prices are perceived by customers.

Remain flexible. Be prepared to adjust prices based on market conditions and customer perceptions. Stay informed about industry trends, economic factors, and customer feedback that could impact your pricing structure. For instance, if competitors adjust their prices, or if there's a shift in consumer demand due to economic changes, a reassessment of your pricing strategy may be required.

Regularly evaluate sales data and financial performance metrics to determine whether your current pricing aligns with your business goals. By being proactive in monitoring and adjusting your pricing strategy, you can ensure it remains effective in driving sales while also meeting customer demand.

Chapter Highlights

- Price for Profit—building sufficient profit into your pricing is essential for covering business costs, taxes, and owner distribution (or wages) and ensuring the long-term sustainability and growth of your business.

- Market Research—study competitor pricing and industry demand to set competitive and profitable prices.

- Analyze Expenses—factor in both overhead and direct costs to ensure that prices cover expenses and yield profits.

- Pricing Models—choose from strategies like cost-plus, value-based, competitive, penetration, and premium pricing to match your business goals.

- Continuous Monitoring: Regularly review and adjust pricing based on market trends, customer feedback, and financial performance.

Chapter Fifteen

Budgeting

A budget acts as a roadmap for your small business, helping you anticipate challenges and navigate the future with clarity and confidence. By outlining your projected income and expenses, you can strategize resource allocation, optimize cash flow, proactively plan for tax obligations, and achieve your financial goals.

Budgeting will allow you to build an emergency fund. While it doesn't benefit your immediate cash flow, having this reserve will come in handy when the unexpected occurs, such as losing a major contract or facing an unexpected employee departure. The emergency fund enhances your resiliency, which is essential if your business is going to survive and thrive in the long run.

An emergency fund is an important and active step in your financial process. Neglecting this step may be tempting, but it will catch up to you eventually. Start small: consider setting aside $100 at a time. Ideally, aim for two to three months' worth of cash reserves to keep you prepared for any financial hiccups that may arise. By prioritizing this fund in your budget, you're not just safeguarding your business; you're also positioning yourself for sustained success in the future.

In addition to an emergency fund, a well-crafted budget is a valuable tool to assist with the following:

- Debt Prevention and Reduction—through expense monitoring and proactive cost-cutting measures, you can prevent unnecessary debt and allocate resources more effectively.

- Problem Solving—it serves as an early warning system, alerting you to potential issues before they escalate, allowing for timely corrective actions.

- Financial Forecasting—projecting future revenue and expenses will help you plan for upcoming periods and guide business strategy.

- Cash Flow Planning—by predicting slow periods, you can ensure the availability of funds required to maintain operations and meet financial obligations, avoiding cash shortages.

- Reinvestment for Growth—a budget guides you on how to reinvest profits: growing your team, upgrading equipment, or making other investments.

- Goal Setting and Motivation—by setting financial targets and milestones, you can motivate your team, fostering a sense of purpose and driving progress toward shared success.

Crafting Your Budget

Don't let the perceived complexity or rigidity of budgeting hold you back. Invest the time to create a comprehensive budget, and you'll gain a powerful tool that offers clarity, direction, and a foundation for sustainable growth.

A budget is set up like your P&L. You can follow these steps to create your budget. After you do this once, the ensuing budgets will become easier:

1. Identify and Forecast Income Sources—begin by listing all revenue streams, including sales, services, and other income sources. Carefully review and forecast these based on the previous year's figures, making adjustments for changes like new products, discontinued services, and new contracts. Stay realistic and don't overestimate based on your high hopes. An unrealistic budget is worthless.

2. Categorize and Estimate Expenses—use past financial records to estimate expenses as accurately as possible and avoid the risk of underestimating or overestimating your costs.

   a. Fixed Costs—list recurring expenses that remain constant (e.g., rent, utilities, insurance, salaries).

   b. Variable Costs—account for expenses that fluctuate based on sales and production levels (e.g., COGS, raw materials, commissions), considering how these costs scale with revenue.

   c. One-time Expenses—allocate funds for unexpected costs (e.g., equipment repairs, new technology purchases) to avoid financial strain.

   d. Taxes: Don't neglect to factor tax obligations in your budget.

3. Calculate Profit—subtract your estimated expenses from your projected revenue to determine potential profit. If negative, revisit your cost structure to discover areas to cut; if positive, plan for how to reinvest those funds for growth.

4. Set Savings Goals—allocate a portion of your income to your emergency fund, building financial resilience and supporting future growth.

5. Monitor and Adjust Regularly—continuously review your budget, adjusting as needed to optimize spending, cut costs, and maintain financial stability.

Taking the time to create a detailed budget helps you anticipate challenges, control cash flow, achieve your goals, and support the long-term viability of your business. Your small business deserves this level of financial planning and strategic foresight.

Crafting Your Budget Without Historical Data

You're likely reading this book at the beginning of your new business venture, and you don't have historical data to use to create a budget. Many small business owners make the mistake of neglecting to create a budget when starting their entrepreneurial journey. Don't let the lack of past data stop you; a well-crafted budget should be a top priority.

Research similar businesses in your industry for estimates to guide your planning. What follows is a step-by-step guide to building a budget, even if you're starting from scratch:

1. Estimate Startup Costs—identify all initial expenses required to launch your business (e.g., licensing fees, equipment purchases, starting inventory, renovations).

2. Project Operating Expenses—estimate your ongoing monthly or annual operating costs (e.g., rent, utilities, insurance, payroll, marketing).

3. Forecast Revenue—use market research and sales projections to estimate your expected income.

4. Include Contingencies—plan for unexpected costs or revenue fluctuations by building a buffer into your budget.

By following these steps, you can create a solid budget for your new small business, even without historical data. Remember, it's okay if you get it wrong! This is just a starting point, and it will take some trial and error before you get the hang of it. Review and update your budget as needed.

How to Use Your Budget

Effectively utilizing your budget will improve your ability to run a successful business. Once you have created your budget, actively engage with the numbers, and use them to guide your financial decisions. To use your budget effectively, take the following actions:

1. Commit to the numbers. A budget is worthless and a waste of time if you don't put in the effort to work toward your goals for both revenue and expenses. A commitment to the budget will increase your chances of meeting your goals.

2. Use your budget! Don't create it and set it aside. Utilize the budget when deciding how much to spend on something. Get in the habit of asking, "Is this in the budget?" Remember, your budget is your guide, so let it guide you.

3. Once you have the basics in your budget, you can play with the numbers. What if sales increase by 5 percent, you lose your largest client, or you negotiate lower costs from suppliers? As your business changes, make changes to your budget.

4. After establishing a master budget for the overall business, you can use this data to create more specific budgets for different departments, projects, or product lines.

5. Lastly, and most importantly, review the actual versus predicted amounts. Be disciplined to review the budget regularly to see how the company is meeting (or not meeting) goals. At a minimum, the budget should be reviewed annually, but I recommend doing it monthly and quarterly. It can be done by comparing it to your P&L.

Comparing the actual financial performance against budgeted figures allows you to do the following:

- Evaluate Performance—determine how well the company is meeting its financial goals and objectives.

- Discover Trends—recognize patterns in financial performance that may require strategic adjustments.

- Improve Planning—use the insights gained from variance analysis to refine future budgeting and forecasting processes.

- Control Costs—monitor and control operational expenses more effectively by pinpointing where overspending occurs.

Create a report comparing your budget to your P&L, including these key elements:

- Budgeted Figures—this column displays the planned revenue, expenses, and profits for the period based on your financial goals and projections.

- Actual Figures—this column shows the actual revenue, expenses, and profits recorded during the period.

- Variance Analysis—this column calculates the difference between the budgeted and actual figures, highlighting discrepancies. Variances can be expressed in both dollar amounts and percentages.

When reviewing this report, identify the categories in which you were under budget and those in which you were over budget. For those categories with a variance, determine the reason. Ask yourself, "Why has the actual performance deviated from the budget?" The answer may include unexpected costs, higher or lower sales, changes in market conditions, or operational inefficiencies.

Being under budget may mean that you can hire additional team members, invest more in team development, or purchase new software. If you are over budget, it indicates that your spending has exceeded the originally planned amount. This is a sign to look closer at the issue and solve it before it becomes a chronic problem for your cash flow.

If your budget is in line and on track with the actual numbers from your P&L, ask yourself, "What actions should I maintain to keep the business steady?"

The Marketing Group
Budget
Dec 1, 2024 to Dec 31, 2024

Income	Buget	Actual	Variance
Services			
Consulting revenue	$44,000.00	$48,500.00	-$4,500.00
Content creation	$33,000.00	$31,000.00	$2,000.00
SEO services	$11,000.00	$13,750.00	-$2,750.00
Social media management	$19,000.00	$11,950.00	$7,050.00
Total services	$107,000.00	$105,200.00	$1,800.00
Total income	**$107,000.00**	**$105,200.00**	**$1,800.00**
Cost of services			
Billable hours	$9,000.00	$12,000.00	-$3,000.00
Total cost of services	**$9,000.00**	**$12,000.00**	**-$3,000.00**
Gross profit	**$98,000.00**	**$93,200.00**	**$4,800.00**
Expenses			
Advertising & marketing	$2,500.00	$2,500.00	$0.00
Contract labor	$1,975.00	$2,375.00	-$400.00
General business expenses			
Bank fees & service charges	$75.00	$75.00	$0.00
Continuing education	$100.00	$330.00	-$230.00
Memberships & subscriptions	$100.00	$128.00	-$28.00
Total general business expenses	$275.00	$533.00	-$258.00
Insurance	$250.00	$250.00	$0.00
Legal & accounting services			
Accounting fees	$500.00	$500.00	$0.00
Legal fees	$500.00	$489.00	$11.00
Total legal & accounting services	$1,000.00	$989.00	$11.00
Meals	$400.00	$328.45	$71.55
Merchant fees	$5,938.95	$5,938.95	$0.00
Office expenses			
Office supplies	$100.00	$78.25	$21.75
Shipping & postage	$20.00	$12.83	$7.17
Total office expenses	$120.00	$91.08	$28.92
Payroll expenses			
Benefits	$2,749.55	$2,749.55	$0.00
Payroll processing fees	$128.00	$128.00	$0.00
Wages	$53,834.62	$53,834.62	$0.00
Total payroll expenses	$56,712.17	$56,712.17	$0.00
Rent	$680.00	$680.00	$0.00
Software & technology			
Hardware	$350.00	$345.16	$4.84
IT services	$475.00	$475.00	$0.00
Software licenses	$600.00	$593.25	$6.75
Website & hosting	$100.00	$84.28	$15.72
Total software & technology	$1,525.00	$1,497.69	$27.31
Supplies	$100.00	$79.23	$20.77
Taxes paid	$6,983.82	$6,983.82	$0.00
Travel			
Airfare	$750.00	$639.25	$110.75
Hotels	$550.00	$506.25	$43.75
Meals	$300.00	$239.79	$60.21
Taxis & shared rides	$100.00	$74.21	$25.79
Tolls & parking	$50.00	$25.00	$25.00
Total travel	$1,750.00	$1,484.50	$265.50
Utilities	$375.00	$349.37	$25.63
Total expenses	**$80,584.94**	**$80,792.26**	**-$207.32**
Net operating income	**$17,415.06**	**$12,407.74**	**$5,007.32**
Other income			
Credit card rewards	$50.00	$85.39	-$35.39
Interest earned	$30.00	$35.62	-$5.62
Total other income	$80.00	$121.01	-$41.01
Total other income	**$80.00**	**$121.01**	**-$41.01**
Net income	**$17,495.06**	**$12,528.75**	**$4,966.31**

Chapter Highlights

- Budget Purpose—acts as a roadmap, guiding businesses to anticipate challenges, control cash flow, and allocate resources

- Debt and Expense Management—helps prevent debt by identifying cost-cutting opportunities and handling expenses effectively

- Forecasting and Planning—projects future revenue and expenses, guiding investment and long-term growth strategies

- Expense Categorization—includes fixed costs (e.g., rent, utilities), variable costs (e.g., materials, commissions), and one-time expenses (e.g., equipment repairs) to ensure comprehensive budgeting

- Profit Calculation—subtracts estimated expenses from projected revenue to determine potential profit and plan for reinvestment or cost-cutting

- Consistent Comparison of Budget vs. Actual Performance—monitors progress, spots patterns, and allows for changes to stay aligned with financial goals

Chapter Sixteen

Tax Time

Tax season is dreaded by most. It's a common source of stress, anxiety, and frustration for small business owners. The process of gathering your financial documents and ensuring compliance with complex regulations can feel overwhelming, especially for those without a dedicated accounting team. A sense of dread pervades small businesses as tax deadlines approach, and the owners worry about mistakes that could lead to penalties or audits.

For this reason, it's important to manage your tax obligations proactively *throughout* the year, not just during filing season. Include taxes in your budget (as mentioned in the previous chapter). Maintain meticulous bookkeeping records and regularly consult with your tax professional to ease the burden when it comes time to file. Ultimately, if you prioritize accurate bookkeeping by implementing the processes outlined in this book, you can head into tax time feeling organized and prepared.

Year-End Review

Before compiling documents and generating reports for your tax professional, conduct a year-end review of your financial records.

If you have maintained consistent bookkeeping throughout the year, most of your records should already be current; however, some aspects may be deferred until year-end. Even if you have an accountant overseeing these processes, ensuring the accuracy of your financial data for tax purposes remains *your* responsibility.

Here are the parts of a year-end review:

- Bank and Credit Card Accounts—confirm all bank accounts and credit card accounts are reconciled to their respective statements. If this has been kept up monthly, confirmation should be quick and easy.

- Loan Balances—verify that the balances listed on your balance sheet align with the final year-end statements. (Discrepancies often stem from a failure to record interest expenses.)

- Accounts Receivable and Payable—review outstanding invoices and bills, and adjust as needed for uncollectible receivables and unpaid bills.

- Inventory—perform a physical inventory count to compare against recorded inventory totals, enabling the reliable calculation of COGS and year-end inventory carryover. (Refer to Chapter 7 for further information on inventory.)

- "Ask My Accountant" Category—check this category in your COA, and review all transactions assigned to it throughout the year. Collect the relevant details and include them in your list of questions for your tax professional.

After completing the above steps, it's time to prepare your financial reports and documents for your tax professional. Once you do this, no further adjustments should be made to the books.

Document Checklist

- P&L

- Balance Sheet

- Payroll Records—including W-2 and 1099 forms for employees and contractors

- Asset Purchases, Sales, and Disposals

- Previous Year's Tax Returns (if applicable)

- More Detailed Information (if required):

  - Cash Flow Statement

  - General Ledger

  - Bank Statements

  - Credit Card Statements

  - Merchant Account Records

  - Loan/Financing Documents/Statements

  - Invoices, Receipts, etc.—documentation for business expenses

- Relevant Business Information:
  - Business Entity Type/Federal Classification— sole proprietorship, partnership, corporation, etc.
  - Employer Identification Number (EIN)

Next, compile a list of questions or concerns. Start by adding the transactions/queries from your "Ask My Accountant" category to the top of your list. Along with other issues or items needing clarification, consider discussing the following suggested questions and topics with your tax professional:

Are there recent tax law changes that affect my business?

Ask about new deductions, credits, and regulations that may impact your tax situation and overall financial planning.

Am I taking advantage of all the deductions and credits I'm eligible for?

Inquire about common deductions specific to your industry, for example, equipment purchases and home office expenses.

Do my assets need depreciation or amortization expenses added to the books?

Ask about depreciation and amortization schedules for fixed and intangible assets.

Should I make estimated tax payments?

Discuss your expected income and tax liabilities to determine if quarterly estimated payments are necessary to avoid penalties next year.

Is my business structured in the most tax-efficient way?

Ask if your current business entity (e.g., sole proprietorship, S corp, C corp) is optimal for minimizing taxes or if restructuring might be beneficial.

What documentation should I keep and for how long?

Be aware of record-keeping requirements and retention periods for tax compliance so that you maintain the documentation supporting your deductions and credits.

What steps should I take now to prepare for next year's taxes?

Discuss strategies for long-term tax planning, such as retirement contributions, succession planning, improved cash flow management, and other changes to refine your tax situation for the following year.

How can I improve my bookkeeping and accounting process?

Seek advice on streamlining financial record-keeping to make tax time easier and enhance your overall tax situation.

Are there deadlines I need to be aware of?

Clarify tax filing and payment deadlines to avoid late fees and interest, including employee and contractor tax forms.

Are there any red flags that could trigger an audit?

Ask if anything in your financials or tax filing practices might increase the likelihood of an IRS audit.

After you have met with your tax professional and they have reviewed your books, your bookkeeping may require some adjustments. This could be recategorizing transactions to more appropriate accounts, adding asset depreciation expenses, or correcting an overlooked error. If your tax professional has access to your bookkeeping software, they may perform these adjustments for you.

Once these adjustments are made, your bookkeeping is final for the year, and your year-end financial reports are ready to be utilized for tax filing.

Depending on the items in your business (and the accounting software you use), your tax preparer may perform a year-end close for certain accounts on your COA. This involves reconciling balances and closing out revenue, expenses, and net income into the retained earnings account. This process ensures that each new year starts with zero balances on the P&L. The net income (or loss) from the previous year will be indicated in the retained earnings account. Profit for the year increases retained earnings, while a loss decreases it.

At year-end, owner investments and distributions may also be adjusted or closed to be shown in the retained earnings account. This confirms that the balance sheet correctly reflects the owner's contributions to and withdrawals from the business during the accounting period.

Chapter Highlights

- Year-round Preparation and Collaboration—proactively manage tax obligations throughout the year with meticulous bookkeeping and regular consultations with your tax professional to ease the stress of tax filing and avoid issues.

- Year-end Review—confirm that all financial records (e.g., bank reconciliations, loan balances, accounts receivable/payable, inventory) are accurate.

- Necessary Documents—gather required documents, including the P&L, balance sheet, payroll records, and previous tax returns.

- Consultation Questions—prepare questions for your tax professional about recent tax law changes, eligible deductions, asset depreciation, estimated tax payments, and tax-efficient business structure.

- Bookkeeping Adjustments—be prepared for your tax professional to make adjustments to your books to finalize your year-end financial reports.

- Year-end Close—understand the process of closing out revenue and expense accounts into retained earnings to start the new year with accurate balances, reflecting profit or loss from the previous year.

Chapter Seventeen

Wrap-up

As we conclude, it should be clear that bookkeeping isn't just about preparing for tax time; it's about ensuring the long-term survival and growth of your venture. Financial mismanagement, especially poor cash flow, is one of the leading causes of small business failure. You cannot outrun or outperform financial chaos. By building a strong financial foundation, you can avoid common pitfalls and develop your business strategy based on reliable information.

Throughout this book, we've covered the essentials of small business finance, from understanding basic accounting principles to interpreting financial reports. By integrating these practices, you will gain control over your cash flow, make informed pricing and budgeting decisions, and be better equipped for tax time.

As Warren Buffett said, "Accounting is the language of business." Knowing this "language" assists you in navigating and succeeding in the business world. Financial literacy is an ongoing process, and no matter where you are in your business journey—whether you're just starting or years in—there is always room to improve. Stay proactive, seek professional guidance, and continue refining your financial strategies.

With the tools and knowledge gained here, you are well on your way to achieving sustainable success and reaching your business goals. We'll wrap up with ten actionable tips that support you in maintaining control of your finances and setting your business up for long-term success.

1. **Maintain Accurate Records in a Timely Manner**
   Keep consistent and detailed bookkeeping to avoid financial errors and ensure tax compliance. Reconcile your books by the fifteenth of the following month to stay on top of it and reduce time spent digging through old receipts.

2. **Separate Business and Personal Finances**
   Create separate bank accounts and financial records for your business and personal finances. This distinction helps you track expenses more effectively and simplify tax filings.

3. **Outsource When Needed**
   Consider hiring a bookkeeper or accountant before your financial operations become overwhelming. Your time is better spent growing your business than handling detailed financial work.

4. **Understand the Accounting Equation**
   Master the basics of assets, liabilities, and equity. These core concepts form the foundation of your balance sheet and comprise your business's financial health.

5. **Regularly Review Financial Statements**
   Review your P&L, balance sheet, and cash flow statements consistently. Keeping a close eye on your finances prevents cash flow problems and helps you

address issues before they become major setbacks.

6. **Price for Profit and Stay Flexible**
Be certain that your pricing strategy covers all costs *and* generates a profit. Revisit and adjust your prices when needed to stay competitive and adapt to changing market conditions.

7. **Set a Realistic Budget**
Develop a budget that reflects both short-term needs and long-term goals. Regularly adjust it based on actual performance to better control costs and meet financial objectives.

8. **Set Aside Money for Taxes**
Allocate a portion of your revenue to taxes throughout the year. This preparation prevents you from being caught off guard when tax season arrives.

9. **Adjust Your Chart of Accounts as You Grow**
As your business evolves, update your COA to accommodate new revenue streams, costs, and inventory categories. This promotes accurate financial reporting and better decision-making.

10. **Collaborate with a Tax Professional**
Work with a tax advisor throughout the year to stay compliant with tax laws, maximize deductions, and optimize your financial strategy. This helps you avoid penalties and potentially reduces your tax burden.

1. https://www.bls.gov/bdm/us_age_naics_00_table7.txt

2. https://www.uschamber.com/co/start/strategy/why-small-businesses-fail

3. Covey, Stephen R. *The Seven Habits of Highly Effective People: Restoring the Character Ethic*. New York: Simon and Schuster, 1989.

Take Control of Your Business Finances

Scan for your FREE download of The Small Business Finances Toolbox or visit tools.thejoyofpursuit.com/financetoolbox

Tools designed to assist small business owners in establishing financial operations. Including:

- Small Business Startup Guide

- Starter P&L Template

- Starter Balance Sheet Template

- Financial Management Checklist (Monthly, Quarterly, Annual)

- Guide to Choosing a Tax Professional

Index

For additional topics and detailed explanations of key concepts, be sure to check the List of Terms in Chapter 3. This index serves as a quick reference to help you find information on the most important topics and navigate the book efficiently.

About the Author

Amanda J. Painter
Owner/Operator, Joy of Pursuit

Amanda is known both personally and professionally for her consistency, clarity, and commitment. Her practicality and focus allow her to keep an accurate perspective on life and business. She is level-headed and gives attention to the necessary priorities without distractions slowing her down. Amanda is an action-taker with a well-thought-out plan of attack in hand.

Throughout her work history, Amanda has built a reputation as a dependable and dedicated team member. She began her career in accounting but grew to discover she also has a passion for the people side of business with Human Resources. With extensive experience in small businesses, Amanda is driven to help entrepreneurs thrive. She understands the challenges of starting a business—demanding work, high stress, and uncertainty—but also deeply appreciates the joy of building something from the ground up and turning dreams into reality.

Despite years of working for a publishing company, Amanda never thought she would write a book. Now as an author, she focuses on empowering small businesses through her work. Her first release, *The Team Solution Series: HR Coaching to Grow Teams and Profit,* is a comprehensive four-part series offering actionable implementation plans to navigate the entire employee journey. Combining her exceptional organizational skills with deep HR expertise, Amanda provides practical solutions to improve efficiency, strengthen teams, and help small business owners succeed.

Amanda lives with her two children at the foothills of the Smoky Mountains in Tennessee. She has a love for the outdoors and gardening, especially cultivating flowers. Among her greatest joys is watching her children grow and supporting them as they pursue their passions.

Connect with Amanda

thejoyofpursuit.com/workwithus

linkedin.com/in/amandajpainter

READY TO HIRE?

Whether hiring a bookkeeper or growing your team, the Hiring Process Toolbox simplifies the process.

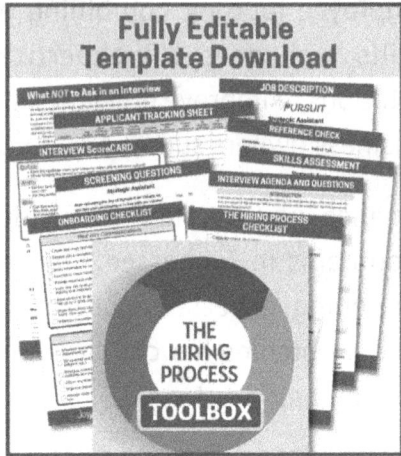

What's Included:
- **Hiring Tools:** Checklists, applicant tracking sheet, customizable job description templates.
- **Evaluation Resources:** Screening questions, skills assessments, evaluation scorecard.
- **Interview Support:** Agendas, questions, compliance tips.

Optimize your hiring process and find the right talent with ease. Purchase now and start building your dream team!

thejoyofpursuit.com/store/p/hiring-toolbox

Tools to establish financial operations and take control of your business.

- Financial Starter Kit
- Employee Expense Management
- Inventory Management System
- Invoicing & A/R Solutions
- Contractor/1099 Payment Monitoring
- And more!

Discover all the financial tools Joy of Pursuit has to offer.

thejoyofpursuit.com/store/finance

41% of small business owners handle HR themselves.

21% rely on employees who juggle HR with other tasks.

Are you part of the
62% without dedicated HR support?

The HR Course for Small Businesses provides 38 tools for managing the entire employee journey.

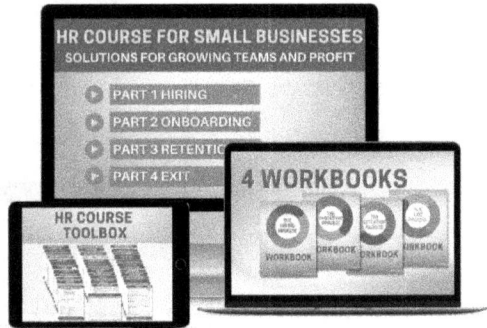

HR COURSE FOR SMALL BUSINESSES
SOLUTIONS FOR GROWING TEAMS AND PROFIT

PART 1 HIRING
PART 2 ONBOARDING
PART 3 RETENTION
PART 4 EXIT

HR COURSE TOOLBOX

4 WORKBOOKS

- **Hiring:** Attract and screen top candidates.
- **Onboarding:** Engage new hires from day one.
- **Retention:** Build a thriving culture.
- **Exit:** Ensure smooth transitions.

Invest in your team's success.
thejoyofpursuit.com/hr-course

Feeling Overwhelmed by Your Company Finances?

If your bookkeeping feels chaotic
or uncertain, you're not alone.
A financial assessment will review your
systems for accuracy and efficiency.

Our assessment includes:

- Review of accounts, reports, and reconciliations.
- Analysis of P&L, balance sheet, and cash flow.
- Detailed report on areas for improvement.
- Actionable steps to streamline bookkeeping.
- Insights into your financial health.

Stop stressing about your books.
Gain clarity and confidence.

Start your assessment today!

thejoyofpursuit.com/store/p/assessment

www.ingramcontent.com/pod-product-compliance
Lightning Source LLC
Chambersburg PA
CBHW071552210326
41597CB00019B/3210